Eliminate the Chaos at Work

Eliminate the Chaos at Work

25 Techniques to Increase Productivity

Laura Leist

WILEY

John Wiley & Sons, Inc.

Published by John Wiley & Sons, Inc., Hoboken, New Jersey.
Published simultaneously in Canada.

Designations used by companies to distinguish their products are often claimed as trademarks. In all instances where John Wiley & Sons, Inc. is aware of a claim, the product names appear in initial capital or all capital letters. Readers, however, should contact the appropriate companies for more complete information regarding trademarks and registrations.

For general information on our other products and services or for technical support, please contact our Customer Care Department within the United States at (800) 762-2974, outside the United States at (317) 572-3993 or fax (317) 572-4002.

Wiley also publishes its books in a variety of electronic formats. Some content that appears in print may not be available in electronic books. For more information about Wiley products, visit our web site at www.wiley.com.

ISBN 978-0-470-87899-6 (cloth); ISBN 978-1-118-03042-4 (ebk);
ISBN 978-1-118-03043-1 (ebk); ISBN 978-1-118-03044-8 (ebk)

Printed in the United States of America.

10 9 8 7 6 5 4 3 2 1

To my fiancé, Robert Strasser,
who joined me on this journey
and provided his technology expertise to this book.
I love you!

Contents

Acknowledgments

I am grateful to so many individuals who helped make this book possible. Our clients and seminar participants provide many opportunities for me and our company Specialists to solve their office productivity and organization challenges. Each client brings a unique situation and encourages us to continually devise custom solutions to eliminate their chaos at work.

I thank my editor at John Wiley & Sons who reached out to me to inquire if I would be interested in writing a book on office organization and productivity. Thank you, Matt Holt, publisher, for the opportunity to collaborate with Wiley on this project.

Early in my career, I learned that I can't do it all and that I must delegate and trust the amazing employees I've hired for their expertise. I am grateful for each of you for your amazing gifts and skill sets you offer to our clients. Thank you to each of you for believing in me and being part of our team.

As much as I wanted to write a book on productivity in the workplace and office organization, I did not want to add one more thing to my plate in 2010 when this manuscript was written. I had to consider that during this time I was still co-managing our practice, working with clients, speaking around the country, planning a wedding, and serving as the president of the National Association of Professional Organizers (NAPO). At the urging of Robert Strasser, my fiancé and our Business Systems Consultant, we figured out a way to make it all possible—agreeing that we would postpone our wedding until 2011. I tried to convince Robert to co-author the book with me, but he wasn't interested, instead choosing to play a more behind-the-scenes role in the process and take on many more responsibilities at home so I could focus my time on writing. Thank you, Rob, for sharing your expertise and insights and for your love and support—I know this book would not have been possible during this time if it wasn't for you. Now, let's go plan our wedding!

Introduction

By picking up this book, you have made the decision to either be more productive at work or work in a more organized environment. Now the question remains: Where do I start? It's a question you need to answer as you begin this process. Your definition of working productively or being organized may be entirely different than the next individual's—and that's okay.

It doesn't matter what industry you work in, or what your job title is; all offices can be broken down into four areas that usually require streamlined systems and processes to be created and maintained. While not every office will require work in all four areas, you need to identify at the onset which ones need improvement, so that you're clear about the goals you want to accomplish. Making statements like "I need to get organized" or "I really wish I knew how to be more productive" will get you nowhere if you do not understand exactly what is standing in your way or which areas need the most help.

These four areas are as follows:

1. Paper: This may include paper management systems, paper flow, and filing and retrieval systems.
2. Electronic Information: Any information stored electronically, such as documents, customer information, photos, and graphics.
3. Stuff: Anything that must live in the office that is not paper.
4. Time Management: The desire and ability to manage your time and prioritize tasks to ensure that you meet deadlines and achieve goals.

Now that you are aware of these areas, you should be easily able to identify which ones need the most help. Most individuals with whom I consult have identified more than one area; however, few people need to transform them all.

The beauty of this book is that you don't need to read it from cover to cover in order to make progress and see results in your office. You can simply turn to one of the four sections and use the information as your guide as you begin to create and implement your new systems. Once you've completed an area, you can move on to another section.

Whether you are an employee, business owner, CEO, or someplace in between, you can execute the information, concepts, processes, and the 25 techniques I've introduced in these pages to fit your needs on a daily basis. You might also figure out somewhere along the way that your coworkers or employees could benefit from this information and these efforts as well. I encourage you to be a catalyst for change in these areas; the more productive your coworkers or employees are, the more positive will be the impact on the bottom line.

25 Techniques to Increase Productivity

1. Identify problem areas up front and set yourself up for success. (Chapter 2)
2. Learn how to manage your actions and choose to spend your time. (Chapter 3)
3. Identify time wasters and implement solutions to eliminate them. (Chapter 4)
4. Develop strategies for accomplishing the most important action items each day in order to meet your goals and complete projects on time. (Chapter 5)
5. Implement an action item task management system, and use it daily to help you manage priorities and time. (Chapter 6)
6. Use the 20-minute rule when entering tasks into your electronic task management system. (Chapter 6)
7. Standardize on one electronic task management system. (Chapter 7)
8. Devise systems to plan your day, week, month, and year. (Chapter 8)
9. Conduct and participate in productive meetings. (Chapter 9)

10. Make time for time management maintenance. (Chapter 10)
11. Implement one or several paper management systems for your office, depending on your needs, including Daily Action Center™, Reference System, Operational or Archival. (Chapter 11)
12. Get in the habit of eliminating paper and information immediately if not needed or after the purpose has been served. (Chapter 12)
13. Use the 10-step process to turn paper piles into files. (Chapter 13)
14. Use the PAPERS™ method daily. (Chapter 14)
15. Design the paper management structure first, and then create the labels. (Chapter 15)
16. Develop and implement strategies to help alter behavior and habits that will reduce your feeling of information overload. (Chapter 16)
17. Implement file naming convention best practices. (Chapter 17)
18. Implement version control for your electronic documents. (Chapter 17)
19. Implement strategies to help you control e-mail, implement a system to keep track of it all, and eliminate the vast quantity of messages in your inbox. (Chapter 18)
20. Understand the questions you should ask and answer these questions before you purchase your next mobile device. (Chapter 19)
21. Connect to your files and applications securely from anywhere via the Internet. (Chapter 20)
22. Organize and share notes, thoughts, photos, and ideas in a way you can find them. (Chapter 20)
23. Find out if a CRM is right for you, and have all of the answers when it is time to implement one. (Chapter 20)
24. Implement a disaster recovery plan for your electronic data. (Chapter 21)
25. Use the Eliminate Chaos 10-step process as your guide to create the organized spaces you desire in your office. (Chapter 22)

1 | How Long Will It Take?

If I had a dollar for every time someone asked me, "How long will this process take?" I might not need to work at all! In all seriousness, however, this question is almost impossible to answer definitively. My response is usually "It depends." Indeed, it *does* depend on four factors that I'll describe in detail in the pages to come. I've always found it fascinating that someone can call and inquire about our services, explain in great detail the extent of the work that needs to be done and how long they've been working that way—and then expect what our specialists have termed the "four-hour miracle." If this work could truly be completed in a mere four hours, I can guarantee you that the individual would've already taken the steps to create these systems and would now be using these processes on a daily basis. But of course, it just doesn't work this way.

Just as I was preparing to write this book, I gave a talk to a roomful of women business owners. The topic touched a bit on time management, paper and information management, and several Outlook® tips that I guaranteed the attendees would save them time on a daily basis. A few days after this seminar, one of the participants e-mailed me and inquired as to how I could help her with her paper and information management systems in her office. She was embarrassed that she had let her office go, with stacks of paper and information everywhere. Since she was only a few weeks away from bringing some new employees on board, she decided she needed to set a good example in the hopes that her employees might also implement these systems—and start being productive right out of the gate. I listened for quite some time as she discussed her needs, past challenges, and how she was thirsty for change but lacked the knowledge and ability to do this on her own. My team and I identified her priorities: to begin with paper management systems and then move on to electronic information at a later date. As we continued to discuss her project in some detail, I began to visualize what I would see when I met with her a couple of weeks later. This time, my new client did not ask me how long her project would take; instead, she told me: one day. I was rather surprised to hear that estimate from someone who had claimed to have never had a good paper management system and never filed anything. I was even more surprised that she thought we'd still have time left at the end of the day for me to answer her Outlook questions.

When our conversation ended, I prepared several documents and e-mailed them to her in preparation for our first meeting. Shortly after I sent the e-mail, I received a reply informing me that creating the paper filing structure, sorting all of her papers, and getting everything filed would take us just three hours. Perfect, I thought to myself, another individual expecting the nonexistent four-hour miracle.

Part of me wanted to ask my client why she wanted our expertise when she was now telling me how to do my job and how long it would take. I wondered how she would react if one of her clients told her how long it was going to take for her write a comprehensive estate plan.

We all have our area of expertise. The most important thing is to do what you are good at and then delegate the rest or hire experts to help you with specific projects. For example, I am not particularly good at graphic design. I see the value of hiring a designer who understands my business and can work with me to create the image we desire to portray. I would never attempt to do this on my own; furthermore, I would be embarrassed to tell my designer how long it will take him to design my new website template or create business cards, stationery, and other marketing material. Rather, I trust that we will collaborate on the project to reach the desired outcome I've hired him for.

The bottom line is this: When you decide that you need to get organized, work more efficiently, and eliminate the chaos at work, you must understand that it's a process, not an event. Don't set yourself up for failure by thinking you can solve all of your problems in four hours—or even a single day. I don't want you to be disappointed, so while this is certainly doable, you need to shift your thinking somewhat. After all, consider how long your office has been like this or how long you've done things a certain way, and allow enough time to change old habits, implement new systems, and use them regularly to ensure they are working. In the end, you're creating a new work-style. This work-style is a conscious choice you make to use daily.

As you begin to work on your projects, here are the four factors that will help you determine how long your project will take:

1. **How much time you are willing to commit to working on this project on a daily or weekly basis.** Let's face it; it's going to be a challenge to make the time during your day for this project. The key phrase here is *make the time.* You will never find the time for this project; you must purposefully incorporate it into your schedule. It will be more time-consuming when you start, but once you've designed and implemented your new systems, you will move on to the maintenance phase—which will become part of your work-style.

2. **How focused you are on the task at hand.** Losing focus to check e-mail, answer the phone, have a conversation with a coworker, or leave the project area to put something in another part of the office will require additional time for you to pull your focus back to the task at hand.

3. **How large the project is.** Maybe you have 60 bankers' boxes of documents that must be sorted, organized, and some placed into archives with the rest filed into a newly created filing system. Or perhaps you have six filing cabinets with four drawers each, full of documents you've never looked at and know you need to cull but can't do so without spending time looking at each client file. Maybe you have just a couple of desk drawers of project files that you need a better system for. Can you see how different each of these three paper projects is? Until you can identify the scope of the individual project, it will be a challenge to determine the amount of time necessary to complete the task.

4. **How quickly you make decisions.** The ability to make quick decisions will have a tremendous impact on how long your project will take. Disorganization and clutter—whether visual, electronic, or mental clutter—are all the result of delayed decisions.

Now that you understand the four factors that determine the length of the project, you are one step closer to answering the question: "How long will it take?" Only *you* can answer this question, unless, of course, you hire a professional to work with you to accomplish your goals.

2 | Biggest Mistakes

Technique #1: Identify Problem Areas Up Front and Set Yourself Up for Success

Now that you are aware of the four areas of the office where productivity can be improved and how long it's going to take, it's important to recognize some of the mistakes that are fairly easy to make along the way. Don't let yourself fall into one of these traps; I've seen them happen time and time again with our clients. This is your opportunity to identify potential problem areas up front and set yourself up for success.

Confusing Being Busy with Being Productive

Problem: Everyone is busy; not everyone is productive. There is a big difference between these two. Stop for a moment and think about a recent conversation you had with a coworker or friend you hadn't seen in a while. Chances are that you reply, "I've been busy" when they ask how you are. But what does this really mean? What have you actually accomplished? Every day, there are going to be things that you must do and things that you want to do. These two categories of tasks are completely distinct from one another.

Solution: Take time each day to identify the three most important activities that tie back to your goals you plan to accomplish. These activities will often be the least fun and are usually time-consuming; that's why it's easy to neglect them and do those easier, more fun, or less time-consuming tasks first—just to be able to cross something off your list. This is exactly how you fall into the trap of being busy but not productive. Always have a plan at the end of the day for the following day; if you wait until the next day to determine your must do's, something will inevitably come up to distract you from carrying out these undertakings. There's no limit to how many must do's you should try to accomplish in a day. I selected three to provide you with a feeling of accomplishment, rather than the sense that "I got nothing

9

done today" because your list was far too long and your goals were unrealistic . . . which brings me to the next mistake.

Setting Unrealistic Goals

Problem: You bite off more than you can chew in a given amount of time or undertake a project for which you do not have the required skill set. The client to whom I referred in the previous chapter thought she was signing up for the four-hour miracle to organize her entire office at work. Upon our arrival at 8 A.M. the day we were scheduled to work with her, she proclaimed that we should be finished by lunch and able to tackle her home office that afternoon. While I know that I work fast, I secretly grinned. After all, if it was that easy and quick, my client would've done the work already herself! In fact, several times throughout the day, our client stated how great it felt to be able to accomplish so much in such a short amount of time, because every time she tried to do this on her own, she got stuck and never finished anything. We were wrapping up her work in her office by 3:30 P.M.

Taking into consideration the hour lunch break, we calculated that the office took us not just 7 hours to organize, but 21—because there were three of us focused on her project all day: the client, one of our consultants, and me. The unrealistic goal she set that day was part of the reason she had not been able to accomplish this project on her own. During these 21 hours, we set up three new filing systems: one for all of her marketing materials, one for all of the client files, and one for all of the files that related to the operation of her business. We did a lot of editing of both the marketing and operation files to pare them down to what was current and in use during the process; in fact, I lost count of how many trips we made to the locked shredding bin. We organized the stuff in her office and left her with a few items to take home and to return to other areas of the office. While we called it a day at 3:30, we had run out of time to address her electronic needs.

Solution: Be realistic—even exaggerate—when determining what you can accomplish in a given amount of time. If you think something is going to take four hours, plan for eight—even if you can't do all eight hours at one time. You will also need to prioritize what the biggest obstacles are that are hindering your ability to be productive at work or that need to be accomplished to work on a future project. Of the five areas our company covers, this particular client wanted to work on four: Time Management, Paper Management, Electronic Information Management, and the stuff. We helped her set a realistic goal of accomplishing the paper management systems and the stuff in her office—since she had pulled everything out of all drawers and off work surfaces. I knew that once there were systems in place for the paper and her office was organized, we could get to the electronic information and time management piece at a later date.

Hiring an Assistant to Help Get You Organized

Problem: You think that an assistant will magically make you more productive and organized. I've seen countless CEOs, VPs, managers, supervisors, and entrepreneurs fall right into the assistant trap. Eventually, you will find yourself in a position where you are more productive because you will be able to delegate tasks, some of which may be the "want to's" that you do not *need* to do. This frees up your time to work on action items that help you attain your goals and complete your projects. You may face a big challenge here: Though you have a vision for how this individual is going to help you accomplish your goal of being more productive or getting organized, you've not yet defined exactly what that vision looks like. In order to accomplish these goals, you need documented systems and processes to use on a regular basis. You need to understand these systems or processes yourself at some level, because when your assistant decides to move on to other opportunities, *you* are going to be responsible for continuing to operate and knowing how to use them in order to train your next assistant quickly. Don't fool yourself into thinking your assistant is going to be able to look at the big picture, understand how the business operates, and be able to design, implement, and maintain these systems independently; this is not an assistant's area of expertise. Assistants, no matter the level (executive, administrative, or personal) will be frustrated with this process and will quickly become annoyed if you expect them to develop these systems in a vacuum without your input or expertise. Assistants excel at *maintaining* these systems—which is the last step of the 10-step process.

Solution: Start with a well-defined job description and understand exactly what you are asking this individual to do for you. This will allow you to ensure you've hired the right person with the skill set you need. A job description should include the responsibilities, as well as the abilities needed to perform the job successfully. After all, if you can't define this, how will you be able to hire someone to assist you? If, for example, computer skills are a big component of the position, develop a short test to ensure they can do what they say; actions speak louder than words on paper. It's better to hire slow and fire fast than to hastily fill the position because you are overwhelmed.

Once your assistant has started, make certain that you are spending enough time to review existing systems and processes, answer questions, and bring your new assistant up to speed on the job functions. If this is a newly created position, you'll need to budget much more time to work with this individual to design and implement the systems that will support you, your team, or your company. The single best way to know that your assistant understands the systems, processes, and routine tasks that you're asking him or her to perform is to have your assistant write an operations or procedures manual for the job function. You accomplish three things by having the assistant write this manual (or update an existing one): (1) you know that your assistant understands all of the responsibilities and how to accomplish the tasks, (2) you have a manual that you can use as a starting point for the next individual you hire, and (3) you have something to fall back on in case you are left having to do the job in the interim, and you can't remember all of the steps involved with a specific task.

Lack of a Customer Relationship Management System—or Not Using the Systems You Have

Problem: I frequently see this problem with solopreneurs, entrepreneurs, and small businesses. There is either no central repository for client information—everyone keeps customer information on their individual computers—or no one has invested the time to customize the software to track client information or train employees on how to use the software. A multitude of problems can ensue: You fail to establish a history of e-mail or phone conversations; you lack the ability to do follow-up in a timely fashion; it's difficult—if not impossible—to pull together a marketing campaign; you have no idea how your customers or prospects heard about you, something that can help you determine if you're spending your marketing dollars wisely; and you run the risk that employees take their customer information with them when they walk out the door or that an IT person who does not know the data's importance simply wipes it off a computer.

Solution: Implement a customer relationship management (CRM) system for your organization. Though this is an investment of both time and money, your ROI here will *far* outweigh the costs of doing nothing. There are many CRM software solutions available that you can customize for your business needs without having to build a proprietary solution. But before you hastily jump in and purchase any software, you need to analyze your business processes. You must understand how you want to use the data you capture and what output you want from the software; this will allow you to determine what the inputs need to be and put you in a better position to customize the system for your specific needs. You should also pay particular attention to cloud-based CRM solutions; some of these will forbid or make it extremely difficult and costly to get your data out, should you desire to move to a new application in the future. Before you fully invest in a CRM system, consider what your exit strategy from that system might be as your business requirements change over time. You will also want to understand how your CRM will interface with other software solutions you are currently using and what the challenges may be when syncing the data to mobile devices (should you choose to do so).

Losing Focus

Problem: You lose focus on the task at hand and then confuse this lack of focus with an inability to get organized. Let's say, for example, that you've decided it is time to organize all of the stuff in your office. You're following the 10-step process that I describe later in the book, so you've set aside the time for this project, but then quickly you become sidetracked by e-mail and phone calls. This trap is an easy one to spot. However, one that's a bit trickier occurs when you're distracted by something you find in your office. You might decide that you need to take action on that item immediately and then fail to return to the task at hand. Maybe you find a project file or book that you've been meaning to return to a coworker or replace in a central filing system. Once you arrive at your coworker's office, you might end up having a conversation—or, worse, being asked to complete yet another task that you hadn't expected. Because of this disruption, you fail to continue working on the project you started.

Solution: Don't confuse losing focus with the inability to organize what you were working on; in such situations, you simply get off track. One of the most effective ways to remain focused is to ensure that you've set aside enough time to accomplish your project. Realize that it may indeed be too large to accomplish all at once and that you may need to break it down into several steps that you can undertake over a period of time. For example, let's say that you need to go through the contents of two bookshelves, a credenza, your work surface, and the floor. You can break these down into five separate projects and concentrate on one area at a time; one day, you focus on one of the bookshelves, and another day, you tackle the floor, and so on. Another tactic you can employ is to set aside items to be returned to other locations or individuals. Establish a place in your office for these articles, and take the time to return them only once you're done working on the specific area. This will give you peace of mind that any conversation or additional work request that comes up along the way will not inhibit your ability to complete your project in the time you set aside to accomplish it.

Delayed Decisions

Problem: A tendency to delay a decision or an inability to make a decision will always lead to clutter. Clutter comes in many forms, both visible and nonvisible. A real estate agent client of mine once referred to organizing her office as *deferred organization*. I loved this term, because it explained exactly what had happened in her office—which, in the end, was truly the outcome of a series of delayed decisions. She explained to me that real estate agents refer to homeowners who have deferred maintenance on their homes, which then causes other challenges. The visible clutter is easy to see (no pun intended) and comes in the form of all of the stuff in your office. As defined in the introduction, *stuff* is anything that must live in the office that is not paper. Nonvisible clutter comes in two forms: electronic and mental. Though your computer might not appear to be disorganized when you first look at it, you can quickly determine upon closer examination how your e-mail, electronic files, customer information, or even the icons on your computer desktop are in disarray. Mental clutter—which is somewhat less apparent—is the result of failing to establish an efficient system for making decisions or capturing all of your action items. In the absence of having tracking systems in place, you will end up with mental clutter and are likely to feel stressed and overwhelmed—not to mention the fact that you're probably going to forget to do something important at some point.

Solution: This solution is easier said than done. I'm not going to sugarcoat this one; you need to be able to make quick, sound decisions and *move on.* Let me provide you with an example or two. Let's say that you receive a brochure for an upcoming conference or seminar you may want to attend. You can't decide at the moment if you can attend, based on reasons such as your schedule, budget, or whether management will approve. So you set the brochure down on a pile of papers—and before you know it, you've piled more stuff on top. You have now lost sight of the brochure and its reminder for you to make a decision at a later date—and before you know it, you've either missed the early bird rate or the opportunity to attend at all.

What if instead of setting that brochure down on a pile of stuff, you made a note of it on your calendar that you needed to make a decision by a specific date—or you added this item to your list of discussion points for your weekly manager meeting? Establishing a location for items that still require a decision allows you to keep them in mind, since you have a reminder on your calendar or action item list. Delayed decisions about the stuff in your office—such as books, tchotchkes you've collected, or excessive amounts of office supplies (just to name a few)—will lead to clutter quickly. You need to ask yourself some questions to help you determine if the items in question still serve a purpose. For example, do the books still have relevant information to which you refer? And if not, is there another way to obtain this information at a later date? Do the tchotchkes have a sentimental value, or are they still in the conference bag you've been storing them in since your return from the meeting three years ago? You need to decide which ones are truly treasures, and which are just trash. In my opinion, office supplies are a strange phenomenon. So many people hoard them in their office but never use what they have. Keep a supply on hand that you will use, and return the excess to the supply room or supply area—something that will reduce both supply costs and waste. I'm sure you get the idea; the better you become at making quick decisions, the less visible and nonvisible clutter you will have.

Shopping First

Problem: You shop before you determine what your needs are. Shopping is actually step 8 in the 10-step process—not step 1, as many people assume. For example, purchasing office furniture before you understand your space and work needs may result in an overabundance of difficult-to-return items. Acquiring an iPhone®, BlackBerry®, Android, or Windows® mobile phone before you determine how all of your systems will work together—and what you hope to accomplish with the device—may set you back several hundred dollars, a lengthy contract, and a large expense for an IT professional to piece it all together if you are not fortunate enough to have an IT department at your disposal. Buying various office organizing supplies such as containers, drawer organizers, and magazine files may lead to wasted time and money before you know the space measurements for these products, just what you will ultimately be organizing, and how much you will actually organize.

    Solution: Resist the urge to shop first, and instead do your due diligence in the area that you are working on. Don't buy a new mobile device based on the store salesperson's recommendations; they don't understand your business and the systems you use. Instead, consult with your IT department or hire a business systems consultant who can analyze your requirements and make the appropriate recommendation. If you are furnishing a new office, you may actually save money in the long run by hiring a space planner to work with you. He or she can determine your workplace needs and help you purchase the appropriate furniture the first time around. If you just need a few containers and organizing supplies to corral the stuff in your office, purchase these during step 8 of the 10-step process. You'll be sure to buy only what you need the first time around, thereby saving yourself both time and money.

Failing to Seek the Appropriate Professional Advice

Problem: You are trying to resolve a technical inefficiency that is out of your scope of knowledge. You consult someone you deem more knowledgeable in this area, for example, the PC desktop support person you or your company uses. However, this person truly doesn't understand the entire scope of the business need and how all of your systems work together. This is one of the most common problems we see in our practice. For example, we worked with a small business—about 60 employees across five locations—that was using POP e-mail. They struggled to collaborate, had no way of sharing contacts or scheduling meetings, and were often forced to delete e-mail in two places: once on their computer and once on their mobile device. While they had an outsourced desktop support IT professional who worked with them on a regular basis, he did not understand the greater company-wide business needs they were trying to resolve. Additionally, he didn't really have a grasp on an enterprise messaging system and resisted migrating the client to this solution—one that would've solved many of their inefficiencies. The company had previously stated that they expected to grow to 250-plus employees within the year and couldn't afford to waste any more time operating in the same manner.

These types of problems happen in all kinds of companies, no matter the size. One of the more common problems we see with a solopreneur or entrepreneur is that they purchase a mobile device based on either their taste or a sales associate's advice, rather than asking the important questions, such as: How do you want to use your mobile device, and what do you need the device to do for you?

Solution: Find an expert with experience in the area in which you need help. Ensure that they know what questions to ask you initially to help define the scope of your project and can narrow down the solutions that will help solve the challenge. Not every IT or mobile phone salesperson is an expert in all areas; it's imperative to find someone who understands how all of your systems are integrated and work together. While this may initially take more time and cost a bit more up front, be assured that if you do this right the first time around, you will save both time and money in the long run.

Time
Management

3 | Can You Really Manage Time?

Technique #2: Learn How to Manage Your Actions and Choose to Spend Your Time

What is time management—and can you really *manage* time? Before I answer that question, you must understand the important distinction I introduced in Chapter 2: the difference between being busy and being productive. Everyone is busy; not everyone is productive. Being productive requires you to engage in activities that *produce results*—which can pose a problem for some people. It's much easier to come into the office and focus on the little, simpler things that don't take very long to do. However, 5 minutes here and 10 minutes there add up. Before you know it, the day is over—and you've not spent any time on activities that produce your desired results.

I will admit that while I was writing this book, there were times when I would've much preferred entering business cards of people I had met recently into our CRM, bookmarking websites I had torn from magazines and journals, or—heaven forbid—even filing papers in our office. While each of these activities was not time-consuming by itself, once I added them up, it could've easily been an hour of my time—an hour that would have been better spent focused on writing this very chapter! Although it may have been less stressful for me to complete these less challenging activities, it was a more productive use of my time to have our client services assistant take them off my plate or to put them off until a later time when I had already spent my two hours a day working on this book. So you see, sometimes even productive people fall into time traps. There are, in fact, so many potentially time-wasting activities, that I will devote the next chapter to this subject. But for now, here are a couple of examples of *busy* versus *productive*.

Time Trap Examples

The social media time trap is an easy one to fall into. Spending 5 to 10 minutes a day tweeting relevant content to position yourself as an expert in your field—in an effort to sell more products, get hired to speak, or gain media attention—is a *productive* use of social media. Telling the world that you had a bagel for breakfast, where you are having lunch, or jumping from one person's profile to the next for fun is not a productive use of time. The same could be said for LinkedIn. Posting relevant content or performing searches for others with whom you can build advantageous professional relationships is an effective use of your time. However, it's easy to get sucked into jumping from one profile to another and reading irrelevant content that isn't going to aid you in making progress on your desired results.

E-mail is another all-too-common time trap. While it certainly speeds up the way we deliver information and documents, it's entirely too easy to get sucked into e-mail exchanges and spend your whole day there. For example, I have seen individuals take an hour or more to compose e-mail because they had to write and rewrite the content to be just so. In many of these cases, a five-minute phone call could've produced the same outcome—perhaps even with better results.

To answer the question "Can you really manage time?" my answer is no. Ultimately, you choose how you spend your time; once it's spent, you don't get it back. So the real issue here is you need to learn *how* to manage your actions and choose how to spend your time. **Actions that produce productive results lead to the efficient management of time.**

4 | 10 of the Biggest Time Wasters at Work and How to Eliminate Them

Technique #3: Identify Time Wasters and Implement Solutions to Eliminate Them

There are so many potential time wasters in the work environment that, in fact, it would be a further waste of time to list them all here! My intent in citing the ones I've selected here is to help you recognize where these time traps exist—and start finding solutions to them.

Distractions

Distractions come in a variety of flavors—e-mail alerts, phone calls, unexpected visitors, office gossip or politics, and employees who aren't doing their jobs. Every office has a Chatty Patty—the individual (male or female) who loves to talk and is oblivious to the fact that you may actually be trying to get something done. Not only have they potentially wasted 5 or 10 minutes of your time with their useless chatter—but it will now take you even *more* time to pick up where you left off. So in reality, they've squandered about 15 minutes or more of your time. Consider the cost of one 15-minute distraction per day for an entire year for an employee making $50,000. It adds up to 62.5 hours for the year—more than a full week of work!—at a cost of $1,500.00. Multiply $1,500 times the number of employees where you work; the amount of money is *staggering*. This may not matter much to an employee of the organization, unless their productivity is tied to a performance-based pay increase, bonus, or how late they end up staying. I can assure you, however, that *any* manager, company owner, or CFO will not be pleased with this—since this type of productivity waste is costly to any kind of organization.

So what can you do to eliminate this type of distraction? You could confront the individual who is wasting your time; after all, he or she may not be aware of the effect this distraction is having on your productivity. This is the most direct way to confront and put an end to this problem. You could establish and make clear that you've set aside certain times of the day when you're available to talk. The next time he or she drops by, explain that you are in the middle of something and would rather talk later during one of your scheduled discussion times. This less direct approach may require you to have this conversation a few times before Chatty Patty gets the hint. Perhaps your group, department, or office could adopt a policy wherein a certain sign on your door or other symbol on your work surface indicates that you are not available for conversation. If your office has meeting or conference rooms available, you may want to consider doing an hour or two of uninterrupted work in one of these locations. You'll be amazed at what you can accomplish in this amount of time when you are 100 percent focused on the task at hand.

Informational and Unsolicited E-Mail

These are two different types of e-mail. Informational e-mail is what you send when you've copied or blind carbon-copied someone on an e-mail. Always consider who is going to receive a given message before you hit the "reply" or "reply all" button. Does everyone currently listed really need to receive it? Understand the difference between putting someone's name in the To, CC, or BCC field:

TO: The only names that should be in this field are of those individuals that you are expecting to take action on the e-mail's content.

CC: Use this field when you want to keep someone in the loop on the subject matter but aren't expecting a response. You CC someone for informational purposes only.

BCC: Use this field when you want to blind carbon-copy someone on the e-mail that you are sending to someone else and don't want the receiver to know who else you are sending it to.

Even when you put someone's name into the CC field—and are therefore not expecting a response—you are still asking someone to take their time to read the message, which can ultimately lead to a lot of hours wasted each week. That is why you should spend a moment before you hit the "send" button and look at whose names are in each of the fields. Then delete those who don't need the e-mail, or move names from one field to another to let recipients know what you expect them to do as a result.

An unsolicited e-mail could be just that—a solicitation—or it could be that someone added your name to an e-mail list without your permission. While you can't do much to stop your name from ending up on distribution lists at work for work-related e-mail, we can all be respectful and not add people to lists that they did not ask to be added to. In fact, there are laws that prohibit this activity and require the sender to provide a way to opt out of the e-mail list. The bottom line is: Be considerate when sending e-mail. Everyone receives more than they need or want, and it can become a big time waster. Don't be afraid to use the delete key.

E-Mail That Does Not Answer the Questions Asked

One of my biggest pet peeves occurs when I take time to compose a thoughtful, well-organized e-mail that contains questions to which I need a response—only to receive in return an e-mail *without* these answers or with some off-the-wall comment that makes no sense at all. I am then forced to spend even more time trying to get an answer the second time around.

There are people who are skimmers and dodgers when it comes to e-mail. The skimmer is the individual who literally skims your e-mail and either doesn't answer all of the questions or responds with a question about something you already stated that went right over their heads—because they didn't take the time to read. The dodger is the individual who responds with a completely off-topic one-liner and makes no attempt to respond to any part of your message. You can avoid being a skimmer or a dodger in two ways: (1) Slow down and read the e-mail carefully, paying attention to the questions that need answers, and (2) do the sender a favor and eliminate one-liner comments, which I promise the sender will appreciate.

If you use Microsoft Outlook, you can mark your comments with your name, initials, business name, or a combination of these when you respond to a message that needs several questions answered. Here's how to do this, assuming you have Outlook 2010:

- From the File tab, select **Options**.
- From the **Outlook Options** dialog box, select **Mail**.
- Click on the **Stationery and Fonts** button.
- On the **Personal Stationery** tab, ensure that a check mark is placed next to "**Mark my comments with:**"
- In the field next to this check box, enter the text you want to see your comments marked with. For example, I use **Laura Leist—Eliminate Chaos**.
- Press **OK** twice.

The next time you receive an e-mail with several questions, reply to the e-mail at the top part of the message with a "See below." Then, place your cursor at the end of the sentence with the question or comment that requires your response. The minute you press the space bar, your name or initials will appear in square brackets; you can then insert your response. I guarantee that this approach will save everyone time, avoid the tendency to overlook information, and make the sender of the e-mail very appreciative.

See Figure 4.1 for an example of how an e-mail might look.

Not Knowing How to Use the Software Tools You Have

I think it's safe to say that you have been self-taught on the majority of the software applications you use on a regular basis. In fact, you can consider yourself lucky if you were able to take a class to learn some of the tips and tricks. I wish more companies understood that a small investment in training in these applications could go a long way toward developing more productive employees.

Let's take two common programs most of us use at work every day: Microsoft Outlook and Word. During an NSA (National Speaker's Association) conference I attended at the time I wrote this book, one

From: Laura Leist - Eliminate Chaos
Sent: Thursday, August 05, 2010 9:22 AM
To: Erin Greely - Eliminate Chaos
Cc: Robert Strasser
Subject: Quick question re: Paris

Hi Erin,

Please see my responses below.

Laura Leist, CPO, CRTS | Eliminate Chaos | 425.670.2551
Follow me on Twitter

From: Erin Greely - Eliminate Chaos
Sent: Wednesday, August 04, 2010 11:18 PM
To: Laura Leist - Eliminate Chaos
Subject: Quick question re: Paris

Hi Laura,

I've been meaning to confirm again about the specifics of per diem and payment for L's project to make sure I understand and there are no surprises.

The per diem is $75/day (dollars, not Euros). *[Laura Leist - Eliminate Chaos] Dollars.[Erin Greely - Eliminate Chaos] OK.* That will go towards food, drink and transportation? *[Laura Leist - Eliminate Chaos]* Food and Drink only. Transportation is separate.*[Erin Greely - Eliminate Chaos]* OK. I think N will be driving me if I need to travel anywhere too far, anyway. I should be able to get around by foot when I'm off the clock! ☺

For the 2 travel days, I am paid $150 each day, totaling $300 for the 2 days combined? *[Laura Leist - Eliminate Chaos]* You can look at this however you like, but I told L it was $300 travel fee for the days you travel to and from Paris. I didn't consider that is was $150/day, but if you want to think of it that way, it's fine. *[Erin Greely - Eliminate Chaos]* OK. Seems very generous to me!

Then all other hours are clocked as usual in 15 min increments? *[Laura Leist - Eliminate Chaos]* Yes, all worked hours are clocked in 15 minute increments – just like at home. If you're out shopping for boxes, you get paid for that time. Of course you can't bill L for a trip charge since you're not using your own car, but it's my understanding her driver will take you – and since you'll be on the clock during that time, it's time billed to L. *[Erin Greely - Eliminate Chaos]* OK.

Anything else regarding billing or payment that is unusual for this project that I'm not thinking of?*[Laura Leist - Eliminate Chaos]* Not that I can think of. If something comes up, we can discuss when you are back.*[Erin Greely - Eliminate Chaos]* OK.

Thanks for the confirmation,

Erin Greely
Organizing Specialist | Eliminate Chaos | O: 425.670.2551 | C: 206.293.7332
ORGANIZING SERVICES: Business | Residential | Home Offices | Relocations | Seminars

Figure 4.1 Sample E-Mail

31

of the presenters made the following statement: "You don't know what you don't know. Spend five minutes a day learning what a new button or feature is of the software you use." He went on to demonstrate the Format Painter option in Microsoft Word. In case you're not familiar with this feature, it allows you to copy formatting from one place and apply it to another. In other words, you don't have to go through all of the steps to highlight the text you want to format, and select the font, font size, color, underline, and so on; instead, Format Painter lets you do this with just a couple of clicks. The "ahas" in the room were astonishing—something so simple yet overlooked every day on a tool that almost everyone in the room was using! This made a very good case for finding one feature a day on your software application and learning how it may be able to save you time.

Let's take a look at Microsoft Outlook for a minute. I want to share with you one simple idea that will not only save you time and help you be more productive and proactive with e-mail, but also help you manage the volume of e-mail more effectively. If you implement this idea, you will never have to go to your Sent file again, searching for an e-mail that you need to follow up on with someone. Nor will you forget to follow up on a piece of e-mail that is time sensitive.

Flagging E-Mail for Follow-Up before You Send the E-Mail (Based on Microsoft Outlook 2010)

How It Works
1. Open a new e-mail message, or the one you are replying to.
2. Click the **Follow Up** button.
3. Select **Custom**. A **Custom dialog box** opens, as pictured in Figure 4.2.
4. Decide if you will flag the e-mail for yourself, the recipient, or both. From the **Flag to** drop-down list, select what follow-up action you need to take. Your options are Call, Do Not Forward, Follow Up, For Your Information, Forward, No Response Necessary, Read, Reply, Reply to All, and Review.
5. Set your **Start date** and **Due date**.
6. Click the **Reminder** box, and set a day and time for your reminder.

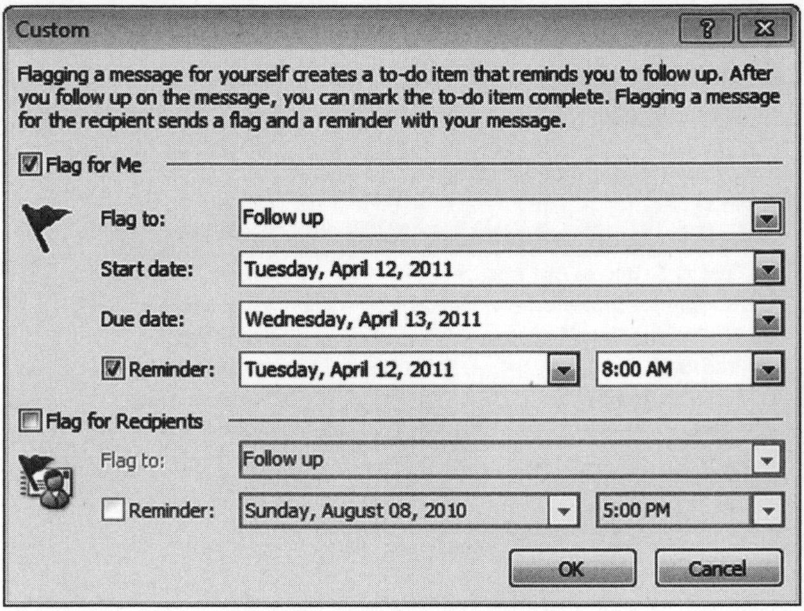

Figure 4.2   Custom Dialog Box

Tip: Set the reminder to appear at the time you arrive at work, so you can review all of your reminders first thing.

7. If you are going to set a flag for your recipient, click in the **Flag for Recipients** box and then set the **Flag to,** along with the reminder date and time.
8. Write your e-mail and press **Send.**
9. Your **Reminder dialog box** will display all reminders, whether they are for a task, appointment, contact, or e-mail. You will notice in the screen capture in Figure 4.3 that each reminder has an icon next to it. This allows you to quickly determine which e-mails require follow-up.
10. If you know that you've already taken care of the e-mail, you can either dismiss the reminder or double-click to open and then delete it.
11. If the e-mail still requires follow-up, double-click to open and forward it back to the recipient to check in—and don't forget to set the reminder flag again before you press Send.

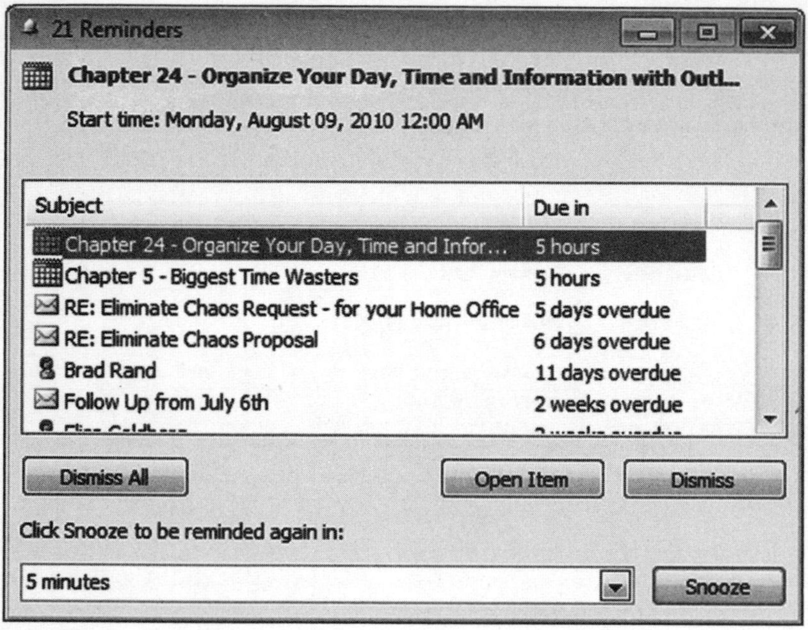

Figure 4.3   Reminder Dialog Box

Tip: If you plan to set a follow-up flag on an e-mail you are sending, I recommend that this be the first step you take when you open the e-mail or begin to respond to one. That way, you won't accidentally press Send without setting the reminder. Once sent, you can't set the flag without resending the e-mail.

Tip: Get in the habit of checking your Reminder box daily. If you don't see the Reminder box, go to the **View** menu and select **Reminders** Window.

Inability to Find Paper Documents or Files When Needed

The lack of a good paper-management system for filing and retrieval is the number one reason that people can't find a document or a file when needed. Simply putting labels on files does not constitute an effective system or structure. Without a system, you may end up creating duplicate folders, several times, for the same information, and then the folders end up in different drawers or locations. You may also be afraid to file it because you will never find it again—and these files can lead to big piles.

In Section Two, you will find information about the various types of paper-management systems you may need to implement, along with examples of filing structures that I hope will provide you with some ideas about how you can begin to create your structure and system.

Inability to Find Electronic Documents or Files When Needed

Electronic files are not immune to the same challenges as paper documents. Again, the problem is in the structure and system—or lack thereof. However, this time waster is less obvious because it is a non-visible form of disorganization and clutter. Whereas you can see all of the piles of paper in your office, when you look at the computer sitting there—well, you just see your computer. It's only once you try to locate an electronic document and can't find it that you may begin to realize how disorganized and unproductive the filing structure is.

Second only to the lack of a well-organized electronic document filing structure are nonexistent and/or inconsistent file-naming conventions and no version controls. In other words, you or others may have created electronic documents with file names that are irrelevant to the document's content. Additionally, you have no idea which version of the document you should use or which is the most current. You can't always assume that the most up-to-date version of a document is the one with the most recent date. After all, if you or someone else has saved a document to your personal hard drive or My Documents folder—rather than a shared file space—someone else potentially has a more recent version of which you are completely unaware, and to which you do not have access.

One way to alleviate this very common problem is to develop and implement companywide policies that dictate where documents are to be stored, how they are to be named, and how you will track versions of the same document. This will be a huge step toward ensuring that you are not wasting time re-creating lost documents because you could not find what you were looking for.

In Section Three, I provide information and examples of naming conventions and version control.

Scheduling Meetings

Before I founded Eliminate Chaos, I worked at a software company in the late 1990s that did not make use of the calendar scheduling feature of Microsoft Outlook. They opted out of this system simply because they did not have their own Microsoft Exchange server and claimed that it was too expensive. I watched executives and managers roam the halls on a daily basis to find a time when a team of people could meet, and I couldn't believe the amount of time I observed being wasted. Didn't this *also* cost the company a lot of money? As a project manager who needed to schedule a lot of meetings, I knew how much time *I* was going to waste—and how unproductive this was when I had more important projects that needed my time and attention. I decided to do a little study of the annual number of meetings that this group of people scheduled. My findings showed that they were losing approximately $95,000 per year in salaried time in a company that employed fewer than 60 people. It didn't take a lot to convince the CEO—who was also the acting CFO—that installing an exchange server would be a good use of company funds and time.

While technology has changed greatly in the past 15 years, some of the same problems still exist. I continue to work with small businesses that do not see the value in deploying this technology, either through their own Exchange server or via a hosted Exchange solution. This leaves their employees to come up with creative ways to schedule both internal and external meetings. Even if you have a method for scheduling internal meetings with colleagues, you may spend a lot of your time playing phone tag or going back and forth on e-mail, trying to find a date and time that works for everyone. This seems a bit silly, especially when you consider the online scheduling tools available to save time. The problem lies in the fact that there is no common scheduling platform.

One of the online scheduling tools, Doodle, conducted a study in September 2010 on scheduling trends that found that "professionals spend 4.75 hours of an average workweek to arrange on average 8.9 meetings. With the amount of time spent for scheduling meetings in businesses, professionals could take a Friday afternoon off every week." Fifteen hundred people participated in this study—half in administrative roles and the other half managerial staff, in the United States, France, and Germany. The amount of time spent scheduling these meetings equates to an eighth of the work hours. This translates to "230 hours spent simply arranging meetings (not attending them); almost 29 working days or close to six working weeks per year." The study's result—summarized in the pie chart in Figure 4.4—showed that 32 percent of meetings scheduled were done so through e-mail, 32 percent with desktop calendars, and 14 percent with online calendars such as Google or Yahoo! The phone still played a large role at 21 percent, while online scheduling tools resulted in only 1 percent.

One of Doodle's final statements regarding the study was "the way managers and administrative professionals organize meetings is inefficient and wastes time. Meetings are necessary, however we choose to hold them, but what isn't necessary is the amount of time currently spent just to arrange them."

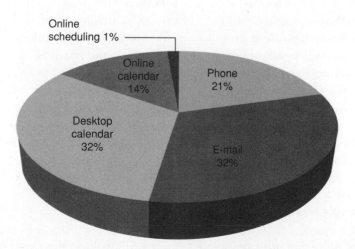

Figure 4.4   Scheduling Trends

Lack of Tools Forcing Work-Arounds

A common yet easily solved problem is the ability to share documents. Instead of e-mailing documents to a coworker—which risks losing documents, using incorrect versions, deleting important information, or trying to determine how several people will easily and efficiently update the same material—there are tools that can be used to share these documents. For example, you could use a shared drive on a server or use a cloud-based file-sharing utility.

Another frequent work-around is e-mailing a contact record to someone from Outlook because of a lack of a shared database or CRM system. E-mailing contacts does not guarantee the accuracy of the information contained in the record, because the original source of the information is eventually lost.

Information Overload

It can be difficult to manage information that comes to you via e-mail, voicemail, texts, tweets, RSS feeds, and social media. This type of information is considered *push* technology—information that is delivered to you without any action on your part. *Pull* technology, on the other hand, requires you to initiate the process to receive information. Pull technology allows you to manage time and tasks more easily because it gives you more control over the information you receive. Push technology saves time because you don't have to go looking for it; however, it can also waste time because you get more than you asked for. Additionally, it takes more time and effort to process the information and decide what you need to keep and how you will store it. In other words, you need to compare the value of the information with the amount of time it will take you to process and store it.

Lack of Documented Processes and Procedures

Every office has processes that need to be followed so there's no need to reinvent the wheel when someone new takes the position. The problem is that not everyone chooses to document these processes. It can therefore become quite time consuming to get up to speed quickly—or sometimes even know what needs to be done—when there is employee turnover.

There are three primary reasons that processes are never documented:
1. Job security: If I document these processes, I am in jeopardy of being replaced.
2. Too time consuming: I have better things to do with my time than maintain a record of these systems.
3. Despise writing: I'm not a good writer, and I have no idea how to go about this task or how much detail to include.

Documents detailing time-consuming, multiple-step processes that are vital to ensure no steps are missed are best written by the person who is currently responsible for them, and future users are responsible for their upkeep. It's absolutely necessary to keep a separate electronic folder for these procedures so they remain together, along with specific file names that include a created or revision date so that everyone is aware of when the last update occurred. A "last updated" date in the document's footer will also prove beneficial to future users. A nearby binder containing the printed procedures is helpful; this gives employees quick access to reminders about tasks that aren't performed often but need to be accomplished the right way the first time to avoid costly and time-consuming mistakes down the road.

Documenting processes and procedures assures business owners, supervisors, or managers that employees understand their roles. Less time will be wasted in the future when new employees must learn each task. My office has two sets of procedures based on job type: one for our specialists and one for the office manager. The amount of time this has saved me over the years when someone new is hired has been a lifesaver. Not only is it easy to provide the binder as part of training but also it helps to cut down on the number of questions asked. Instead, employees immediately answer these themselves by understanding the steps of the policy or procedure. While these kinds of tools will never eliminate new employee training, they ensure that all employees are on the same page and therefore not creating more work for someone else because they did not follow a specific process. Although over the years a few employees have resisted the upkeep, we found that the majority have been grateful to have such a well-documented resource to turn to with questions. In fact, I can almost see the relief on new employees' faces as they learn that they don't need to remember every last little detail—because they know it will be in their procedures binder.

Consider the benefit this would offer you when you are being promoted or asked to shift responsibilities. Though you may still be responsible for training your replacement, think how much faster this could occur if you documented processes to use as the basis of the training. Your transition could be completed more efficiently with more time for your new projects.

So how many of these time traps sound familiar to you—and what can you change today that will immediately improve your professional productivity? The majority of the time wasters discussed in this chapter can be eliminated and fixed within a matter of minutes. Granted, some will take more time, such as learning new tools or documenting procedures. However, because of the time you will have saved yourself, you can spend as little as 30 minutes a week working on these—and still experience a world of difference.

5 | Three Priorities a Day Keep Chaos and Clutter Away

Technique #4: Develop Strategies for Accomplishing the Most Important Action Items Each Day in Order to Meet Your Goals and Complete Projects on Time

Is your to-do list much longer than the time you have available each day to accomplish all of the items on it? If so, you are not alone; this is an all-too-common professional situation. Let's face it: Your inbox will never be totally empty, and your to-do list will never be 100 percent complete. However, you *can*—and must—develop strategies for accomplishing the most important action items each day in order to meet your goals and complete your projects on time. But how do you do this?

The first step is to create a system that you will use and maintain each day that will track your to-dos or, as I like to call them, *action items*. You must have a place where you can store information from multiple sources, including everything you are trying to remember. Inputting this information into a system that works for you will set you up for success and diminish the chance that you'll forget to do something or miss an important deadline.

There are many computer and cloud-based tools you can use to manage your action items, some of which I cover in more depth in Chapters 6 and 7. For those of you who are still a bit reluctant to use an electronic action item management system, there are, of course, paper-based solutions as well. You may even find that your ideal solution is a hybrid of electronic and paper-based systems.

The key to your success is selecting a system that you will actually **use** on a daily basis. It will do you absolutely no good to spend your time implementing a new tool if you don't make use of it; I can't stress this enough. The complaints I consistently hear about these various to-do lists, tasks systems, or whatever you want to call them is that they "don't work."

Our clients express these frustrations because:
- They don't understand the difference between a task and a project and how to use their system for both types of activities.

43

- They didn't spend the time thinking about what they wanted to get out of the system or bother to ask, "Why is this solution for me?"
- They failed to look at the compatibility issues. Does the application only work with a Mac® or a PC? Is the browser compatible?
- They failed to do a needs assessment to see if the tool is appropriate for their needs. This doesn't require anything formal; you just need to write down what you expect this system to accomplish for you.
- They don't sync properly between their computer and mobile device.
- They don't know how to set up and maintain a system.
- They haven't made the time to manage their time and action items.
- They don't bother to look at the system once they set it up, because they feel that it's too overwhelming.
- They spend all of their time trying to find the perfect application to manage their action items, instead of finding one that will manage 80 percent and focusing on the execution of the system.

As I said before, there are many electronic and paper-based tools available; however, it's nearly impossible to find the one application that will ever be the ideal solution for you. The best approach is to stop wasting time and money trying to find this nonexistent perfect solution and instead begin working with a tool you already have. This will put you in a much better position to focus on the system's execution, thereby achieving your desired results. Wouldn't this be a preferable outcome?

Once you have identified your new tool of choice, the next step is to get your data into the system—keeping in mind that your action items may come from multiple locations. After your information is in the system, you are ready to start planning daily action items and being able to identify your priorities. The best time to identify what you plan to accomplish the following day is before you leave work at the end of your day. When you fail to plan for the next day and instead wait until the following morning, you're likely to be distracted by e-mail and voicemail that need your attention, as well as unexpected visitors who drop by your office. Instead, at the end of each day, identify the three biggest priorities you need to accomplish the following day. You may think that this does not sound like much, especially if your action items that need to be accomplished are relatively short tasks. However, homing in on these three action items increases the chance that you'll accomplish them—much more so than when you create a list so long that it quickly becomes overwhelming, causing you to instead accomplish *nothing*. There is no rule that says you can't complete more than three tasks a day, but to begin, just pick the three that are the biggest priorities. You can then use the time you have left to select extra priorities to accomplish.

The end of the day is also a good time to review any notes you have made about additional action items that have come up during the day. What can you cross off the list? What do you need to carry over to the following day? Which action items now need to be recorded in your electronic action item management system? Completing your day with preparation for the following day will set you up for success, eliminate morning chaos, and give your mind a break—since you're not thinking about what you need to accomplish the following day.

6 | Creating an Effective Action Item Task Management System

Technique #5: Implement an Action Item Task Management System, and Use It Daily to Help You Manage Priorities and Time

Technique #6: Use the 20-Minute Rule When Entering Tasks into Your Electronic Task Management System

No electronic or paper-based tools will solve the problem of having an effective action item system unless you *use* the system you create on a daily basis. While it's possible that no perfect application or paper-based tool exists—and that you might not be 100 percent satisfied all the time—if it solves 80 percent of your challenges, then I recommend that you do the necessary implementation, get your action items into the system, and start using it immediately. You must use this system on a daily basis for at least a month to figure out if it's going to work for you. It has been said that a new habit takes about 21 days to form—so give yourself a month and determine what is working and what isn't so you can make the necessary changes. Don't just give up without making the required adjustments; sometimes, you'll just need to do a bit of minor tweaking.

Keep in mind that it's going to take you some time to set up your electronic or paper-based system of choice. You need to ensure that you set aside an appropriate amount of time at the beginning to establish your system and input your data. It's simply not efficient to start using your new system that hasn't been loaded with all of your data; you'll still have to look at too many places and will be left feeling like your system isn't working. If you don't finish setting it up properly, it isn't going work as it should.

Case Study

I once received a call from a very successful CEO and business owner named Kevin who expressed that his to-do list system was not working for him. He explained that he was using Tasks in Microsoft Outlook to manage his action items and needed a better system for managing his activities. On the day we met, Kevin further lamented that his problem with his tasks is that they were all red. If you've ever used the Tasks tool in Outlook, you know that they turn red when they are overdue. While Kevin was well aware of this, the volume of overdue tasks caused him to stop using the system entirely. He, of course, realized what a big mistake this was, as several important deadlines had passed.

He further commented that he knew he could change the due dates so the tasks wouldn't show up as overdue tasks, but he still didn't think this system would work for him. Upon further examination of how he had designed his action item system using Tasks, it was clear that with a few minor adjustments and customizing this system a bit more for his needs, he would still be able to use this tool to manage his daily, weekly, and monthly activities.

Kevin's first challenge came as a result of the way he was viewing his tasks. Not only did most of his 250-plus tasks display in red, but he was using the Simple List view—one of 13 different available options. This alternative displayed one very lengthy list of his tasks—the mere sight of which overwhelmed him. This was only compounded by the number of overdue action items that were appearing.

The first problem we needed to solve was to change how Kevin viewed his action items. I suggested that he perhaps consider the view By Category, which would allow us to further break down into groups (categories) those tasks that were related to one another. He agreed, and so we began to talk about the types of tasks for which he was responsible and came up with the following (partial) list of categories:

- Assistant's Tasks
- Business Development
- Marketing
- Personal
- Projects
- Volunteer Work
- Website Redesign

At this point, Kevin was starting to visualize a different way to view his action items—now By Category rather than in one long overwhelming list! With a list of our categories on paper, we were ready to create them in his master category list and then categorize each task. By the end of our session, we had categorized existing action items, set new realistic due dates—and were able to view his action item list By Category.

Later in this chapter, I will demonstrate the By Category view with Tasks and how you can implement this at work.

Don't Confuse a Task with a Project

The *Merriam-Webster Online Dictionary* defines the word *task* as
(a) an assigned piece of work often to be finished within a certain time and (b) something hard or unpleasant that has to be done.

I define a task as a single action item. While it's up to you to determine whether the task is unpleasant or enjoyable, I would not agree that *all* are "hard and unpleasant," as defined by Merriam-Webster.

A project, on the other hand, is comprised of a series of tasks with start and end dates. One way to differentiate between the two is to follow the **20-Minute Rule:** Put only those action items into your electronic action management system that will take more than 20 minutes to do. You don't want the mere act of creating tasks to become a data entry exercise. The administration of this system should not take longer than the time it takes to complete the task.

I know what you're thinking: "But what do I do with all of those other things that come up each day that I need to take care of and not forget?" A good question indeed! I recommend that you have a pad of paper or notebook where you can quickly write down an action item—all in the same location. If you find that this item never gets done, reevaluate whether it's a priority; if it is, perhaps it's time to put it on the Task list to do at a later date. The idea behind the notebook is to keep you from forgetting to return a call or send someone information they are waiting for. These are relatively short action items that don't need to go into your electronic system, only to check it off later or delete it. Instead of spending all of your time inputting tasks into the system, you need to focus your time on *doing* the tasks. After all, if you spend all your time managing the process, you will never get any actual work done.

Tasks—Microsoft Outlook

Each time Microsoft releases a new version of Outlook, I cross my fingers that they have made this application more user-friendly. I'm still waiting for the company to accept the notion that people might like to be able to prioritize their tasks in terms of more than just a *high* or *low* setting. This just scratches the surface of the long list of enhancements I would like to see implemented in this program, but alas, I am not the product manager. Because Outlook is still the most widely used e-mail client in the business environment, I will share with you some ways that I've helped clients configure Tasks and create a system that will work.

As mentioned previously, there are many ways to view your tasks; the 2010 version of Outlook has 12 predefined views. I have found the **By Category** view to be one of the most useful, as long as you set up a custom category list and don't rely on the standard, predefined colored categories. Editing the Master Category list lets you create your own categories and delete those that serve no purpose. The challenging part for most of us is *defining* the structure of these groups, since there is only one Master Category list that is used with all Outlook's components (such as Contacts, Calendar, Notes, Inbox, and Tasks). Adding to the challenge is the fact that you can't have subcategories or categories for each component of Outlook.

How to Create Custom Categories

1. Think about the type of information you want to categorize. Is it more than just your tasks? Chances are, if you're using Contacts, you will want to classify Contacts, Tasks, and maybe even your Notes and some Calendar appointments. If this is the case, you could end up with a long list of categories, or you could subdivide it by the type of information you will sort. For example, the categories that you want to use to organize your Tasks may not be the same ones you would use to organize your Contacts. Instead of scrolling through a long list each time you want to categorize a contact or a task, you can create your own sections of categories for Contacts and Tasks.

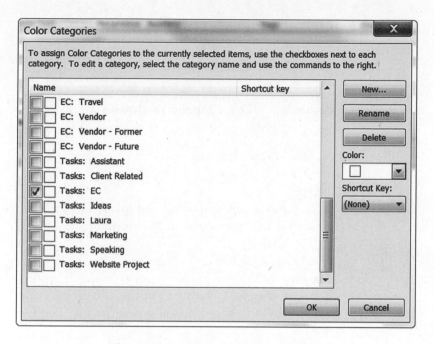

Figure 6.1   Master Category List

2. You can see in the screen capture in Figure 6.1 how I've started each category that I will use with tasks with the word **Tasks:** and just above are the categories I use with Contacts; each beginning with EC:—which stands for Eliminate Chaos. Now I can visually see the separation of my task categories from those I will use with Contacts. Additionally, if I had categories I wanted to use with my calendar appointments or notes, I might start them each with Cal: or Notes:, respectively.

3. Click on the **Categorize** button, as shown in Figure 6.2.

4. Click on **All Categories** at the end of the menu.

5. A Color Categories dialog box opens, like the one seen previously.

6. Select any categories you do not wish to use and press the **Delete** key; then click **Yes**.

Categorize

Figure 6.2 The Categorize Button

7. Click on the **New** button, enter the category name, determine if you want a color associated with the category, and click **OK**.

   Tip: Keep punctuation, spelling, and spaces consistent, or your category list will not display in alphabetic order.

Once you have made your Master Category list, you are ready to categorize your existing Tasks or create new ones. The screen capture in Figure 6.3 displays an example of how I set up and categorized tasks according to specific areas of business, as well as personal use. The **EC**

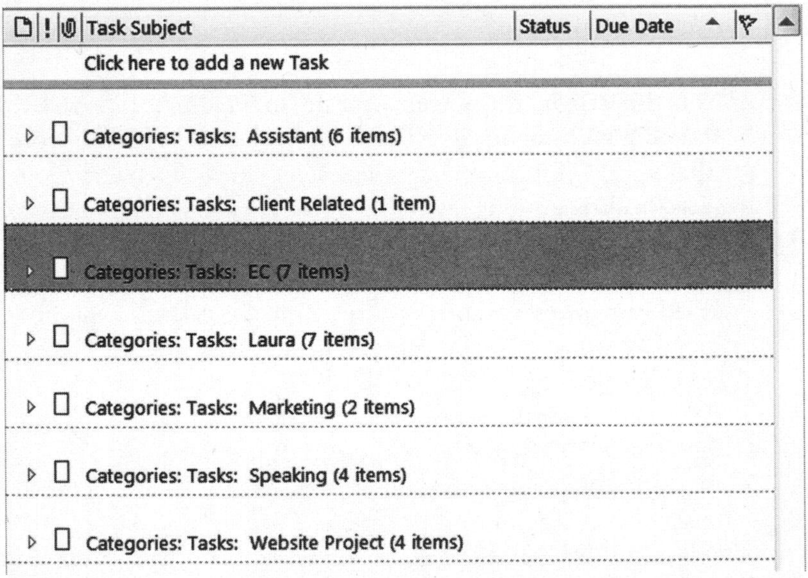
Task Subject
Status
Due Date
Click here to add a new Task
Categories: Tasks: Assistant (6 items)
Categories: Tasks: Client Related (1 item)
Categories: Tasks: EC (7 items)
Categories: Tasks: Laura (7 items)
Categories: Tasks: Marketing (2 items)
Categories: Tasks: Speaking (4 items)
Categories: Tasks: Website Project (4 items)

Figure 6.3 Task Subjects

that appears shaded stands for *Eliminate Chaos;* this is where I put the everyday tasks that must be done.

Once the Category is expanded, you are able to see all of the tasks associated. You can keep the categories that you aren't looking at collapsed and expand only the ones you want to see, as seen in Figure 6.4.

There is much more to Tasks than I have room to describe in this chapter. If you'd like additional information on how to use and customize Tasks, you will find it in one of my Outlook books that are available on our website: www.eliminatethechaosatwork.com.

I would be remiss if I did not share with you several of the other many task management applications available. For that reason, you will find a brief explanation of some of the more widely used tools for both PC and Mac users in the next chapter.

It takes dedication and time—not a particular piece of software or Internet application—to make any effective action item system work.

☐ ! ⑩	Task Subject	Due Date ▲	🏹 ▲
	Click here to add a new Task		
▷ ☐	Categories: Tasks: Assistant (6 items)		
▷ ☐	Categories: Tasks: Client Related (1 item)		
◢ ▉	Categories: Tasks: EC (8 items)		
📋	Write Article for NSA Magazine	None	🏹
📋	Update P&P manual to include note to add signature to Out of Office Messages	Mon 10/4/2010	🏹
📋	Find Someone to Write Bio	Fri 10/8/2010	🏹
📋	Update Professional Photo	Wed 10/20/2010	🏹
📋	Write November Newsletter	Fri 10/29/2010	🏹
📋	Trademarks	Fri 10/29/2010	🏹
📋	Submit Proposal to Speak at NSA Convention	Mon 11/15/2010	🏹
📋	WBENC Certification	Fri 2/25/2011	🏹
▷ ☐	Categories: Tasks: Laura (7 items)		
▷ ☐	Categories: Tasks: Marketing (3 items)		
▷ ☐	Categories: Tasks: Speaking (4 items)		
▷ ☐	Categories: Tasks: Website Project (4 items)		

Figure 6.4   Categorizing Tasks

You can spend your time looking for a better tool or fine-tuning the one you have, but at the end of the day, you won't get much done. No tool, whether paper-based or electronic, will ever be the perfect solution, but the combination of dedication, time, *and* the tool will help you achieve success!

7 | Task Management Applications and How to Use Them

Technique #7: Standardize on One Electronic Task-Management System

In the previous chapter, I talked about why it is so important to create an effective action item system for your tasks. This chapter explores a few of the many applications available for doing so. (Note: I am not being compensated to discuss these applications; they are simply the ones that seem to be the most widely used.) Some are designed as a piece of software; others are Cloud- or Internet-based and can also sync to your computer. There are also a couple of options for those who prefer to use paper.

Applications—Computer and Cloud-Based

TeuxDeux

TeuxDeux is a free Internet application you can access from any computer. There is an iPhone app available for purchase that allows you to use TeuxDeux when you're out of the office; conversely, you can use the browser on your phone to access your TeuxDeux account. To use TeuxDeux's words, this tool was built as a bare-bones application. You'll find that this tool is easy to use and doesn't require much of a learning curve. It displays a five-day view with a list of tasks for each day. While there is no option to number your tasks in order of priority, you can drag and drop tasks in the order you wish to complete them. Additionally, if something doesn't get done on a given day, just drag it forward to a future date.

For those who follow David Allen's GTD® methodology, this application has a Someday section at the bottom of the screen. This is the perfect location for listing all tasks that you will do someday (or maybe never) so that you can get them out of your head and assign them a date in the future. Instead of just making one big long list of

Someday tasks, you can create headings for Someday, such as Personal or Work, and then move them to separate columns. As you add new tasks to the Someday section, simply move the someday task to the appropriate column.

Remember the Milk™

Remember the Milk—or RTM—is a free online task manager that allows you to manage your tasks anywhere. RTM is more complex than TeuxDeux, yet still fairly easy to use. The biggest challenge here is remembering all of the keyboard shortcuts that will help you add, edit, move, prioritize, search, repeat, and postpone tasks (just to name a few!). I like that you can create separate lists for different categories of tasks. This helps you quickly see your tasks in each area and allows you to print only those tasks. However, you can use the All Tasks view to see or print all of your tasks together. You can sort by priority, due date, or task name, regardless of which list you're looking at. One beneficial feature is that RTM automatically generates a completed task list that keeps your tasks even after you've marked them completed. You also have the option to delete these tasks if you don't want to see them again.

You can upgrade to the Pro version of RTM for $25/year to synchronize to your mobile device and receive free access for Android, iPhone, iPod touch®, MilkSync for BlackBerry, or MilkSync for Windows Mobile. If you want to access your tasks off-line, you can install a plug-in for your browser called Google Gears™. I also find it helpful that you can have reminders sent to you via e-mail, instant messaging, Skype, and more at a date and time you predetermine. For example, you can have all of your reminders sent to you the day before they are due at a specific time each day, or you can opt to receive them ahead of time. If you need to share tasks with a project team or your assistant, you can share them by adding them in your RTM contacts; however, they must also have an RTM account. You then e-mail them an invitation to share your list(s). You have the option of selecting the lists you desire to share with them and can also publish your lists for your contacts or make the list public.

RTM also works with iGoogle™, which allows you to manage, review, add, edit, postpone, and mark tasks complete.

Gmail™ Tasks

Tasks is a free application within Gmail. Like TeuxDeux, it is fairly bare bones but not as user-friendly, in my opinion. This tool provides the option for you to create multiple lists, which in effect lets you categorize your tasks and indent a task to create a subtask within each list. While there are no *priority* features, you can move tasks up and down in the list if you want a prioritized list, or sort tasks based on due date. Although Tasks doesn't automatically e-mail you when the tasks are due, you do have the option to e-mail a task list to yourself or others. You can also turn an e-mail into a task so you have the details of something that requires action. Since Gmail is a web-based application, you're able to access your Tasks from your mobile phone using a browser.

Using a task management system with Google becomes more powerful when you combine Remember the Milk with iGoogle. You do this by installing a free Google Gadget™ that allows you to manage your RTM tasks from iGoogle so you have your e-mail, contacts, calendar, and an even more powerful task management system in one place.

Toodledo™

Toodledo is a free online to-do list that you can access with your browser to keep track of your tasks. If you prefer, you can purchase an application for $3.99 to sync it with the iPhone, iPod touch®, or iPad™. You can purchase the Pro or Pro Plus version for $14.95 or $29.95, respectively, to have access to features such as encryption, subtasks, an auto-scheduler, and upload files. Toodledo has numerous features, several of which I will touch on briefly here. The basic concept is to organize your tasks into folders, which you can name based on the type of activity, project, or personal tasks under which they fall. Since one of Toodledo's features is the ability to share your tasks, you can also designate folders as private so that others can't see your tasks in these folders (for example, one in which you keep personal tasks). You always control who has permission to read or modify your tasks in any shared folders, and whether you want to give someone permission to add tasks.

You can also set a due date and a priority. There are five levels of priorities, one being a negative priority that hides tasks that are not an immediate priority. Conversely, tasks that you set as Top priorities will appear in a Hotlist. The Hotlist is a feature that displays tasks that are due soon or have a high priority.

Since some tasks you generate will be recurring, you can set these to repeat daily, weekly, monthly, or yearly. The time-tracking feature lets you gauge the amount of time a particular task takes you. Some tasks may require notes to be completed; you can attach these to your task. If you have notes that don't relate to the task but need a place to store them, the Notebook is the location for this type of information.

While there is a search feature available, there are additional ways to search or sort your tasks that you can use, such as Contexts, Tags, or Keywords. A Context helps you organize tasks by location and/or what you are doing. For example, if you are at work, you can set your contexts to hide personal tasks. Tags or keywords describe your tasks.

If you desire, you can integrate Toodledo with Google Calendar™ and Apple's iCal® to give you a visual reminder of when tasks are due. In addition, you can send yourself a copy of a folder or receive e-mail reminders of upcoming tasks. You can go beyond integration here; if you are using another task management application, you can export your tasks from systems including Microsoft Outlook, Apple iCal, Remember the Milk, and Palm OS® for PDAs, and import them to Toodledo.

There are a couple of third-party applications for purchase that you can use to sync your Toodledo tasks to Outlook. However, I do not usually recommend this, as we've had clients use these applications and subsequently had their tasks deleted or fail to synchronize. Toodledo states that they do not provide support for third-party applications that sync tasks—so buyer beware. David Allen's GTD methodology can be used with this application as it supports contexts; however, you can also implement your own task management system that works for you.

Things for Mac®

Things is a software program that works with the Mac OS®. At the time this book was written, it sold for $49.95, and it syncs with the Things iPhone app that can also be purchased. This application is a GTD application based on David Allen's Getting Things Done® methodology. It is quite simplistic and provides five primary areas in which to manage your tasks: a collection Inbox, Focus, Active Projects, Areas, and People. Using the GTD methodology, the idea behind the Inbox is to have a place to put all of your tasks before they are categorized and tagged. The Focus area is a place to store tasks that need to be worked on today. You have several options for how to group your tasks, whether by project or area of responsibility. Using tags will allow you to easily sort and filter tasks.

Things integrates with iCal, notifies you of upcoming tasks, and works with Spotlight for quick searching.

Todo™

Todo from Appigo can be used with your iPhone, iPad, or iPod touch; you can also sync your tasks using Todo Online. Todo for the iPhone or iPad was about $4.99 at the time this book was written. If you want to be able to sync your tasks over the Internet, it will cost you an additional $19.99 a year.

Todo for the iPhone, iPod touch, or iPad allows you to group tasks by using lists, thus categorizing or grouping certain tasks together to create a project. You can set multiple reminders for these and even protect your lists with a password. The iPad application allows you to download different themes that make your tasks appear in a binder with different paper types that looks like a paper planner on your iPad. Todo supports David Allen's GTD methodology if you use this process to manage your tasks and next actions.

Todo Online gives you the ability to access your tasks anywhere by using a browser on your phone or computer. It will sync your tasks and multiple alerts and also syncs with iCal, Outlook, and Toodledo. If you're going to use Todo for one of these devices, it's a good idea to purchase Todo Online; this way, you know that you'll always have a backup of your tasks and projects should something happen to one of your devices.

Action Method Online

Action Method is a different approach to managing action items through an online application, the iPhone, and even paper products; it provides the ability to work efficiently and increase productivity. With this tool, it all starts with the action steps, also known as tasks. As discussed earlier in the book, a task is a single action item, whereas a project is comprised of several action items. What I really like about this online tool is that you can easily create and manage projects. By using the drag and drop features, you can reorder your action steps and view them by the target (due) date or project.

We all know that not all projects and tasks are created equally. Sometimes you may be working on a task or project by yourself, and other times you may find yourself working in a collaborative nature with others. This tool supports both approaches, as its Delegate feature allows you to assign an action step to another individual—assuming that the other person is also using Action Method. If you delegate an action step to someone, they have the option to accept or reject it. You will be able to see in your list that it has been delegated and to whom. A handy little feature called Nag is used to remind someone that you've not heard from them regarding an action step that you assigned to them. When you've completed an appointed action step, you simply check a box, and a notification appears in the Action Method inbox of the individual who allocated it. While nobody likes to be nagged, the good news is that there's also an Appreciate feature that will let you send kudos for a job well done.

There are several other cool functions this online tool provides. You can track the amount of time an action step takes, use references and backburners, or engage in a discussion. This last one is especially helpful; instead of participating in a lengthy e-mail exchange, you can start a discussion inside Action Method and invite others to participate. This lets you see all of the discussion about a particular action step all in one place. References—such as notes, links, or files related to a particular action step or a project—are also stored within the system. Finally, backburners are for great ideas that aren't quite ready to become action steps. Therefore, you leave them on the backburner to be revisited at a later date. This gives you a place to capture these ideas so they don't slip away.

There are two different plans available for the Action Method. The introductory plan is free but allows you to create only 50 action steps. The premium plan—for $12 a month or $99 annually (at the time of writing)—lets you create an unlimited number of action steps. The premium plan also provides the ability to upload files and attachments that you can share with others or include in the discussions; otherwise, you're left to enter text or add a link to a shared document. The iPhone application is free and will give you the ability to create, manage, and delegate action steps on the go and organize your projects. Finally, there are also Action Method paper products you can use in conjunction with Action Method Online that allow you to record action steps on the go or when brainstorming during a meeting.

Paper-Based Action Item Solutions for Tasks

Some people are more tactile and love crossing things off paper. For these people, there is no better solution than a piece of paper and a pen. There are some pros to this system, such as the fact that paper will never crash, fail to sync, or have its batteries die. There are, however, two very significant cons to paper-based systems: You have no backup when you lose information or spill something on the papers, and you will spend a lot of time rewriting these lists. If you have an aversion to the electronic solutions, you could at least use a journal book or small notebook to track your to-dos. I recommend dividing it into sections based on your action items, such as calls to make or return, work-related action items, personal action items, and so forth. You can use Avery® Write-On™ tabs to divide the notebook and a Sharpie to write your category.

Resist the urge to keep a notebook or journal book full of tasks that you've already completed. Any information that is worth keeping is worth transferring to another system. For example, you should store a phone number or e-mail address where you keep this type of information or bookmark a website link for future reference.

If you prefer something with more structure than a piece of paper or a journal book, the FranklinCovey® planner may be an option for you. These planners are designed to help you keep track of your tasks, appointments, notes, and contacts.

If you are uncertain as to how one of these solutions will integrate best with your existing technology, it might be a good idea to consult with an expert who can look at the big picture and determine if the solution is worth the investment of your time and resources. The cost of each of these solutions is minimal in comparison with the amount of time you could potentially spend undoing or fixing data because it did not sync the way you thought it would.

Whether you choose to use an electronic or paper-based task management system, the key is to find a tool that will work for you at least 80 percent of the time and get all of your tasks out of your head and into the tool of choice. Now you are ready to use this system to help ensure nothing slips through the cracks—and hopefully make you a bit more productive.

8 | Planning Your Day, Week, Month, and Year—Looking Forward and Back

Technique #8: Devise Systems to Plan Your Day, Week, Month, and Year

People often ask me what the best product for office organization is. It's a question that makes me cringe, because there is no *product* that exists that can be the ultimate solution. While product and technology can play a role in the overall solution, they are typically not *the* solution. So my answer to this question is usually "It depends." While I fully realize this is not the answer most people are hoping to hear, it truly *does* depend on several factors—such as the part of your office or workday you're trying to organize and make more productive. We established in the introduction that it's necessary to organize four components of the office to make your workplace work for you—and an important one of these is time management. No matter what, I would *always* recommend that you have some sort of calendar. In fact, it is the one product I will always tell people they need to have in their office.

You would think that having a calendar would be just as important as having a chair on which to sit to do your work. Yet I am frequently surprised to encounter people who don't use calendars to help plan their days. I live by my calendar; as the saying goes in our office, "If it's not on Laura's calendar, it's not going to happen." While I recognize that this may be somewhat of an extreme approach, the system that works for me is one where I put just about *everything* I'm planning to do on my calendar. I want to have a record of what I am going to accomplish each day and to always remain aware of meetings, client appointments, speaking engagements, business travel, vacations, and personal appointments.

The key to effectively planning your day, week, month, and year is to devise a system that works for *you*—one that will capture your activity on an ongoing basis. Though this ultimately becomes the system you maintain on a daily basis, you'll need to establish some of the basics first and figure out exactly what will help you manage your actions on a regular basis.

Techniques to Plan Your Day, Week, Month, and Year

1. **Use *one* calendar.** If possible, use a single calendar for work and personal activities. Though this may not be possible in a corporate environment, it's absolutely necessary for solo-preneurs and entrepreneurs.

2. **Choose an electronic calendar.** I know there will be some who will disagree with me on this point and insist that they prefer their paper calendar. While it's fine to use what works for you, keep in mind that the data you store in a paper planner are not backed up. If you lose it, it's gone—forever. If, on the other hand, you lose a Smartphone, you're out the money; however, your calendar should be synchronized to your computer to provide you with a backup. One of my colleagues swore by her FranklinCovey Planner and paper calendar—until the day her car was broken into and it was stolen. Even though she had heard me speak several times about why I encouraged people to keep an electronic calendar, she had resisted the change. It didn't take her long to make the switch after losing her planner to theft. Keep in mind that you can always print daily, weekly, or monthly schedules if you want a hard copy to keep with you.

3. **Schedule vacations and other time off as far in advance as possible.** It's best to get these items on your calendar as early as possible to ensure you make time for vacation and are able to get the time off that you need. I cherish my time off; because I am self-employed, I take several mini vacations throughout the year, as well as at least one two-week vacation that I use to recharge my batteries. I can usually guarantee that if I don't plan these at least six months in advance (if not further out) that other activities are likely to arise that will make it impossible for me to take the time off—or force me to change plans.

4. **Schedule recurring meetings and other activities in advance.** If your calendar is electronic, use the recurrence feature to schedule as many of these as possible into the future. This limits the amount of individual entries you need to make, and you can always delete or remove one—while leaving the rest on your calendar—if you're not able to attend. Use the notes

section of the appointment to enter information for an up-coming staff, project, or employee meeting. This keeps all of your data in one location and lets you easily print it out before a meeting. It also serves as a reminder for what was discussed during these appointments.

5. **Don't schedule meetings or activities back to back to back.** When you schedule meetings back to back, you do not allow yourself a cushion of time that is needed for the following tasks:

   - File meeting notes
   - Input any tasks as a result of the meeting
   - Prepare for your next meeting
   - Get to your next meeting
   - Check voicemail and return any urgent calls
   - Check e-mail
   - Use the restroom
   - Grab a snack
   - Take a break
   - Eat lunch

   You will read more in the next chapter about how this habit caused one of my clients to consistently have to work evenings and weekends. Make sure you schedule enough transitional time between each meeting and activity so that you don't feel rushed or behind before your day has barely started. You'll be thankful for the time cushion if a meeting runs long or you have an unexpected interruption.

6. **Schedule time for meeting prep and follow-up.** Whether you are the meeting organizer or simply an attendee, chances are that you need to do something to prepare. Arriving pre-pared shows everyone that you value their time as much as you value yours. In the same vein, completing follow-up items af-ter a meeting may be even more important than attending the meeting itself. It may actually take you less time if you can take care of them as soon as possible after the meeting, while they are fresh in your mind. If this is not possible, make sure that you've scheduled time to complete your follow-up tasks. If you say you are going to do something, make a note and deliver by the time you promised to do so. Don't force

someone else—like your boss or employee—to have to ask you whether it's done; they already have enough on their own plates.

7. **Schedule time for administrative tasks.** Everyone has some administrative tasks they need to complete on a weekly basis. However, unless you are in an administrative role, you may not have considered that these may never get done if you don't make time for them. Small business owners and entrepreneurs are notorious for avoiding such vital activities as recording expenses, invoicing, following up with clients, paying bills, and keeping customer information current in the CRM system. Determine the amount of time it will take you to accomplish these activities on a weekly basis, and plan that time accordingly. Better yet, hire someone for a mere 10 hours a week to whom you can delegate these tasks. This makes a great job for a college student or a stay-at-home mom looking for a way to reenter the workforce.

8. **Give yourself a break.** You can't work all day without taking time for lunch and a couple of other short breaks. You will do yourself a favor if you can walk away from your work and clear your mind. You'll come back feeling refreshed and able to concentrate—and significantly better than if you had stayed in your office all day.

9. **Do an end of day, week, and month recap.** Review what you were not able to accomplish at the end of both the day and week, and decide what needs to be moved forward and to when. Before the end of the month, take a few minutes to see if there are any meetings that need to be scheduled or rescheduled and/or any unfinished projects or tasks whose due dates you need to revise. Spending 10 minutes on this activity ensures that you don't accidentally forget anything important that you must carry forward.

Planning your day, week, month, and year is not a time-consuming task. In fact, it should only take you a few minutes each day to keep it current once you develop your calendaring system. The more you are able to plan in advance, the better off you will be in the future when someone asks if you are available to volunteer, undertake a new project, or take a last-minute vacation.

9 | Planning and Participating in Productive Meetings

Technique #9: Conduct and Participate in Productive Meetings

Meetings can consume the better part of your day, yet so many people wonder at the end of the day: How much did I really *accomplish* by attending one meeting after the next? Before you go to another meeting, stop for a moment and consider why you're there in the first place.

- Is it for informational purposes only? If so, can you obtain the necessary information from someone else?
- Is it because you have something to contribute? If so, is there a reason you need to stay for the *entire* meeting? Most people stay because it looks bad to walk out. Plan a politically correct way to exit.
- Are you the one who requested the meeting? If so, what steps are you taking to ensure that it produces the results you need—without the attendees feeling as though their time has been wasted?

Several years ago, I received a phone call from a mid-level manager for a large health care insurance company named Dan. He told me that he needed help managing his time more effectively; he felt as though he never accomplished anything during the day, always took work home in the evenings, and often worked on weekends to get caught up. I reviewed Dan's Outlook calendar for the current month during our first session and could instantly see *why* he felt as though he never accomplished anything: He spent almost every hour of the day in meetings. The majority of his meetings were an hour long, with a couple that were 30 minutes. Most of the meetings were scheduled back to back, with absolutely no time in between to:

- File meeting notes
- Input any tasks as a result of the meeting into his electronic task management system

- Prepare for and get to the next meeting
- Check voicemail and return any urgent calls
- Check e-mail
- Use the restroom
- Grab a snack or eat lunch
- Take any sort of break

Can you relate to his hectic schedule? If so, you are not alone. Dan's challenge wasn't necessarily to better manage his time, but instead how to be more productive before, during, and after all of the meetings he was required to attend. Because Dan also lacked an efficient system for capturing his meeting notes and follow-up actions from the meeting and a place to file his notes for each project, he felt overwhelmed, stressed, and as though he was in a constant state of being reactive versus proactive. By applying several of the following techniques, we were able to free up some of Dan's previously consumed meeting time for activities that produced better results and got more of his own project work done during the day—instead of at night or on the weekends.

Techniques to Implement to Ensure Productive Meetings

1. **Start meetings *on time*.** This shows that you respect everyone else's time. If you continually start meetings late, people will come to expect this and stop arriving on time. Make it clear when you schedule the meeting that it will begin promptly. Sitting in your chair at the start time signals that the meeting is about to begin.
2. **Show up on time.** When you show up late, you are telling everyone in the room that your time is more valuable than all of their time put together—which certainly is *not* the message you want to send.
3. **Make a rule: Last person to arrive takes notes.** This rule will encourage everyone to arrive promptly; after all, who really wants to be responsible for taking notes for everyone?
4. **Lock the door when the meeting starts.** This will send notice to latecomers that the start time is important and must be heeded.

5. **Use an agenda.** Meetings lasting longer than 20 minutes should always have an agenda to ensure that you stay focused and cover the appropriate items. The meeting organizer should create the agenda, which should contain the following information:

    (a) Meeting date
    (b) Meeting purpose
    (c) Project or department name
    (d) Meeting attendees
    (e) Topics for discussion, along with a realistic amount of time to discuss each

    Meeting agendas should be kept electronically in their own Agenda folder for each project or department so they can be referred to if necessary. This way, attendees can eliminate their paper agenda yet still access the electronic version if needed.

6. **Distribute the agenda before the meeting**. Providing the agenda to attendees as far in advance of the meeting as possible will help everyone make better use of time. It will allow time for any prep that may be necessary, rather than catching attendees off guard or risking that people will be unprepared. There are several ways you can distribute this information electronically prior to a meeting:

    (a) Send the agenda as an attachment in an e-mail.
    (b) Send the agenda as an attachment to a meeting request.
    (c) Send the agenda as part of the text in the meeting request.
    (d) Send a link to the agenda that is stored in a shared location.

7. **Keep it short.** Shorter meetings can accomplish just as much as one that is twice as long, especially if you implement these techniques.

8. **Schedule a 45-minute meeting instead of an hour.** Meetings somehow have a way of filling all of the time scheduled, so don't allow this to happen in the first place. You can use the extra 15 minutes to accomplish one or more of the previously listed activities *before* you go to your next meeting.

9. **Don't allow scope creep.** Discussing an unrelated topic is one of the easiest ways to derail a meeting and will only

frustrate and waste others' time. It's another reason an agenda is necessary; it keeps the meeting on topic for everyone. If a topic that isn't on the agenda comes up, put it on the parking lot and return to it at a later date—or address it if there is time at the end of the meeting.

10. **Acknowledge the elephant in the room.** If there is something standing in the way of making forward progress, acknowledge it up front and move on. The sooner and more openly this topic is addressed, the better.

11. **Choose an effective moderator or facilitator.** Someone needs to be responsible for keeping the meeting on topic and moving along. If this is not one of your strengths, enlist someone who can help you run a productive meeting. Observe their tactics and approach for the running the meeting, so that you can learn how to do so yourself more effectively in the future.

12. **Assign a designated timekeeper.** This person is responsible for stating that it's time to move on to the next topic, either verbally or with some sort of buzzer. A timekeeper will discourage someone from dominating the meeting and keep it moving forward.

13. **Conduct meetings while standing.** Sitting in a chair for shorter meetings allows you to get comfortable and consume more time. Could you accomplish just as much standing in less time? Give it a try.

14. **Listen.** Show your respect to the person speaking; you'll expect the same when it's your turn.

15. **Stop multitasking.** Establish a policy of no e-mail, cell phones, texting, or surfing the Internet during meetings. Require attendees to place their phone in the middle of the table, out of reach until the meeting is over. If the meeting is short enough, these techniques should not be problematic.

16. **Show some respect.** Acknowledge others' contributions, and be open to their ideas.

17. **Be prepared.** Don't be caught off guard if someone asks for your opinion or advice. No one appreciates the person who always attends the meeting but never contributes. What's the point of attending?

18. **Don't speak just to be heard.** Speak only if you have something meaningful to add. People stop listening to those who speak all the time but never really *say* anything.

19. **If it's feasible, attend the meeting by phone.** When possible, attending a meeting by phone can save travel time and money on both ends. This valuable time can then be used to accomplish other priorities for the day.

20. **Follow up.** Most meetings are likely to result in several action items. Though everyone should be responsible for their own to-do's, people get busy. They might forget what they were asked to do or forget to communicate that they've completed these items. Designating someone to record action items and post them to a shared document will help ensure completion. However, someone may still need to be named as the follow-up person to remind others of their commitment.

21. **Decline a meeting request.** Though you'll want to proceed with caution here, you must understand that it's not necessary for you to attend every meeting to which you're invited. Review the three reasons for attending from the beginning of the chapter. If it is for informational purposes only, you might be able to obtain the information you need from another individual. Consider what you could accomplish during the scheduled meeting time if you did not attend.

22. **Can the meeting be replaced by a phone call?** Ensure that every meeting you attend or schedule can't be replaced by a phone call. If a meeting is needed later as a result of the call, you can schedule one at that time.

23. **Cancel a meeting.** If you are the meeting organizer and realize that you aren't prepared for it, do everyone a favor and reschedule it. Your colleagues will be grateful that you haven't wasted their time.

24. **End the meeting on time.** Just as you will start meetings on time, you need to end them on time—if not early. Never assume that you can continue a meeting after the scheduled end time; you may not be aware of what attendees have scheduled next. End the meeting early if your agenda is complete; don't continue the meeting just to fill the time scheduled. Everyone will thank you for this.

25. **Send out meeting notes if kept.** If someone is the designated meeting note taker, by all means, share the notes with other attendees, or at least let everyone know where they can find the notes at a later date.

Though several of the previous ideas may be not be new to you, they will hopefully serve as a helpful reminder. If these techniques were used regularly in the workplace, I would not spend the time to write about them.

In my quest to see what others had done to ensure productive meetings at their organizations, I found the following unique ideas that I wanted to share with you.

Techniques from Others

1. **Imagine that your best client is attending the meeting.** Ask yourself, "Would our client think this meeting was productive?" This tends to limit the amount of wasted time on nonessential topics, such as complaining about problems instead of working toward solutions. It also helps keep the focus on getting the most from the meeting rather than veering off on peripheral topics. (Peter Donohoe)

2. **Use a dollar box.** Each time someone is late, she or he puts a dollar in the box. The money goes into a fund for doughnuts, beer, or something else for the entire office. Sometimes, however, a larger penalty may be needed, such as $1 for the first time you're late, $2 for the next, and $4 for each time thereafter. (Mark Herschberg)

Many of the techniques suggested here have to do with time. To that end, a visual reminder of the time coupled with the technique may help make a more productive use of that time. I have found the Time Timer to be a helpful product for meetings during which I need to measure or manage time. This product allows you to literally *see* the passage of time. You set the timer for the length of the meeting or project; then, as the time elapses, the red disk gets smaller, so you know how much time you have left to work with. Clocks show time as a static number, but this product helps you visualize time as a segment. You can purchase their products from www.timetimer.com.

They offer three sizes of their free-standing clocks, an application you can download to your iPhone or iPad, and software that provides several different options for how you choose to display time.

Productive meetings are always possible when you implement the techniques introduced in this chapter. What can you do immediately to ensure that you're running more productive and efficient meetings? Even if you're not the one in charge, you can facilitate a productive meeting by being responsible and respectful of everyone's time.

10 | Make Time for Time Management Maintenance

Technique #10: Make Time for Time Management Maintenance

In this section of the book, you have
1. Answered the question: Can you really manage time?
2. Read about the biggest time wasters.
3. Learned to establish and focus on your top three priorities for each day.
4. Found out how to create an effective action items system that works for you.
5. Discovered new tools and resources for managing time.
6. Established ways to plan your day, week, month, and year.
7. Explored strategies you can implement to foster productive meetings.

The chapters in this section provide a foundation for you to acquire new tools, resources, ideas, and strategies that will help you manage your actions. In turn, you'll produce valuable results that lead to the efficient management of time. Remember how we answered the question "Can you really manage time?" in Chapter 3? I said that although time cannot be managed, it can be used more wisely; to that end, you need to learn how to manage your actions and control how you spend your time.

I hope that you had a few aha moments as you read each chapter and discovered several takeaways to implement immediately. Though it will take you some time to create your new systems and employ the ideas in this section, it's vital that you make it a priority to schedule time to do so. If you can't set aside time to establish these processes, you will never have a complete system that you can maintain on a regular basis. Though there will be a period of transition between your previous systems to your new ones, you will feel disjointed until you have your systems in place.

After you've implemented these systems and undergone any transitions that needed to take place, it will be time for what I call maintenance. This simply means using your tools and systems on a regular basis, and for most people, this takes less than 5 to 10 minutes a day. Maintenance will never go away; it must become a habitual part of your workday.

You will also want to review your systems occasionally to ensure they are still working at their optimal level for you—and if not, make any necessary changes. I recommend that you use this review as an opportunity to take an honest look at what you have put into your system. Are you going to accomplish everything you entered? Have your priorities or responsibilities shifted? If so, your system needs to reflect these changes. Have you neglected to input important projects or tasks into your system? Be sure you make the time to update as needed.

It's not enough to merely create the system; you must also make efforts toward time management maintenance to get the most effective results from the tools you've chosen to use.

II | Paper Management

11 | Paper Management Systems Defined

Technique #11: Implement One or Several Paper Management Systems for Your Office, Depending on Your Needs, Including Daily Action Center™, Reference System, Operational or Archival

Beginning today, I want you to think differently about how you will organize, store, and retrieve paper and information. You most likely feel so overwhelmed by all of the paper and information surrounding you because you may not have taken the time to consider that you really need multiple systems, each with a specific purpose. While it may initially sound like a lot of work to create multiple systems, I guarantee that you will end up saving time and be able to quickly retrieve the information you need at the moment you need it. This is usually what people fear most: not being able to easily *retrieve* information exactly when they need it.

Why You Need to Use a Variety of Systems, Rather Than Just One

I have yet to work with a client who uses just one system to organize paper and information. Most offices with which I work use a combination of the systems defined in this chapter. Some factors that will help you determine which systems you need to create are frequency of use and the type of information to be stored.

Daily Action Center™

A daily action center is a place to store paperwork and other information that you access daily or even several times a day. This location must be easily accessible from your desk area—either in a desk filing drawer or a portable filing box. A transportable daily action center can sit on top of your desk or on the floor underneath.

91

Paperwork for Your Daily Action Center Might Include
- Current project or client files
- Fax cover sheets
- Takeout menus
- Computer entry
- Expense report receipts
- Pending or follow-up items
- Travel files for upcoming business trips
- Bills to pay
- Reading (documents you've printed to read later, not magazines, journals, or newspapers)

Reference System

Unlike the daily action center, you are probably already familiar with the concept of a reference system—which is just another name for a filing system. Though the information you store in a reference system requires no further action in the immediate future, it still needs to be retained. Most people do not enjoy filing, so to eliminate the pain that comes to mind when we envision this task, let's call it what it really is—a reference system—instead.

A document that requires no further action does not automatically become a candidate for the reference system, however. Most of us keep way more paper than we'll ever look at, use, or reference again—so it's best to make a decision before storing it. Here are some questions to ask before placing documents or files in your reference system.

Financial and Legal Questions
Is there a tax-related or legal reason to keep it?
Am I legally required to keep it?
Does it belong to me?
What will it cost to keep, store, and maintain?
Does it take more time and effort to manage than it is worth?
Will this help make or save money?

General or Reference Questions
If I keep it, will I remember I have it?
If I remember I have it, will I be able to find it?

Is this information relevant to me or a coworker?
Is the information still current?
Do I need it? How long do I need to keep it?
If I don't need it, why do I want to keep it?
When can I get rid of it?
Will I refer to it?
Is it a duplicate?
Can it easily be duplicated or created if needed again?
When's the last time I referred to it?
Will I read it?
Do I have time to read it?
Do I have the space to store it?
Is this the best place for it?
What's the worst that can happen if I eliminate it?

Since you won't be accessing your reference information every day, you don't need to make your filing cabinet, rolling file cart, or stacking file boxes as easily accessible as your daily action center. However, you also don't want to place it somewhere so hard to get to that you use it as an excuse to avoid filing. You should go through your reference files at least once annually and determine what can be moved to your archive files to free up space for the upcoming year.

Operational

An operational system may be similar to a reference system; it's a place where you store documents related to your company's operation. This kind of system works well for smaller or individual offices by giving them a single location to file all documents related to running the business.

Files in Your Operational System May Include
- Advertising information
- Business licenses
- Continuing education
- Contracts
- Financial information, such as banking accounts or credit cards

- Insurance policies
- Lease(s)
- Marketing material
- Receipts
- Tax-related documents
- Website information

As you can see, client or project files are not stored in this system. These files are stored separately in their own system, which we'll discuss next.

Client/Customer

Client files are typically stored in one of two places: a central location in the office or—depending on the nature of your work—within your personal work area. Some offices have client files stored in multiple locations. Distinguishing between active and inactive client files helps to determine the location where they are stored. For example, clients with whom you are now working may occupy an entire desk drawer for quick and easy access. They could also live in your daily action center if you don't want to designate an entire area or drawer to these files. Client projects that are completed or no longer active may live either in a designated client or customer system in your work area or in a centrally located spot accessible to everyone in the office.

Project

Project files are typically stored in the work area of the person responsible for the project. Project size and whether they are active will help determine where they are located within the work area. If there is ample filing drawer space, a drawer can be designated for these files. It may make more sense for some people to place active project files in a daily action center. The best time to edit out project files is, unsurprisingly, once they're completed; it is rare you would ever need to keep all related documents once you've finished a project. These files should then be moved to a reference or archived area until the documents can be destroyed.

Archival Systems

Depending on space, it may be necessary to archive some documents and files that need to be kept but are rarely accessed. Some examples of this type of paperwork might include old client files, legal documents, tax-related information, and former project documentation. Because of the important nature of this information, it's critical that you take the proper precautions to ensure that the documents are not destroyed by water, mold, rodents, or yellowing over the years. Document archiving companies store these documents off-site, and many offer digital archiving as well.

Client Examples

To demonstrate exactly how to use these systems in the workplace, I am going to share with you examples of four systems I created for various sized businesses—all in different industries.

Home Health Care Agency—130+ Employees

Problem: Inability to know when contracts were up for renewal. Whether it was for the advertising in the Yellow Pages, their website hosting, IT services, or lease renewal, this company had contracts spread throughout the owners'—and some managers'—individual offices. There was no system in place to show at a glance all of their contractual obligations.

Solution: Locate all of the contracts and centralize them into an operational system to be located in the accounting office. When a contract was finalized, all of the related documents were to be placed in a single drawer dedicated to all company contracts. Additionally, all contracts were logged into an Excel® spreadsheet that lived on their server, and employees were able to look up information about a given contract at any time, from the comfort of their offices.

Certified Financial Planner Who Worked for a Large Financial Planning Corporation

Problem: No system for managing the day-to-day operations of her own business within this company. This particular individual wasn't able to find information when she needed it, and she had similar documents stored in multiple locations. There was no system for managing current client files or keeping track of all of the marketing literature she used to create a new client information package. The only system she did have was an alphabetic system for inactive client files, which lacked the structure to tell her what needed to be in each client file.

Solution: We created two filing drawers for all of her marketing literature, information, and products with a company logo. This allowed her to quickly create a new client packet and cut down on the amount of literature she was ordering—now that she had it all in one, easily accessible place. The second system we created used two drawers for her operational files—anything she needs to run her business. We incorporated most of the operational files previously mentioned in this chapter. This provided peace of mind in that she could quickly locate notes for an upcoming seminar or access the continuing education documentation she needed to maintain her credential. The last thing we did was to review her client system. We designated an entire drawer within arm's reach for her active clients and organized them according to last name first, while inactive client files remained in four lateral filing drawers for her to evaluate and edit at a later date. Armed with several new systems, instead of just one, she didn't have to think about where something was stored; she could now go directly to that system and find what she needed in just a few seconds.

Information Technology Director and Project Manager for a Hospital Division

Problem: Doesn't enjoy filing (seriously; who does?). This person was afraid to let go of documents for fear that they may be needed some day and had more projects than could fit into her current filing drawer space. She was unsure where to store documents for employee meetings or department management so she could locate them quickly. Additionally, she had no central filing areas for her department—so she stored everything in her office.

Solution: We created a daily action center that contained files for each employee, as well as 20-minute projects, reading, and bills that needed her approval. This is a temporary location for her to place information that is needed for her weekly one-on-one meetings with staff, as well as quick projects and bills to keep them from piling up on her desk. Then, when she designates time to review bills or do a quick project, she does not have to go searching for this material; she can just grab the folder and get started. We also used the locking drawer in her desk for the operational—including employee—files. We created another daily action center in a portable filing box that contained current projects she was working on, in order to get them off her desk and floor at the end of the day. We established several portable, hinged-lid project boxes to organize documents pertaining to each completed project that needed to be kept and stored out of the way but did not need to take up the valuable file drawer space that was at a premium in her office.

Manager for Spa with More Than 75 Employees

Problem: Employee files were spread out across too many locations and not locked down—which led to uncertainty about what employee files actually existed. Spa operation projects were piled in several locations throughout the office, and there was no system in place for accomplishing daily activities. The vendor files were in a filing cabinet but not in a working system where employees could quickly retrieve product information for ordering supplies.

Solution: We began by identifying a locked filing location in the main office to house employee files in alphabetic order, last name first. We designed a checklist for the documents that were to live in each employee file, so that a human resource representative could easily review the material and collect the necessary documents needed to complete each file. We then created a daily action center for current projects to remain on top of the desk, since the manager needed a visual reminder of projects that needed ongoing attention. After conducting a major purge of vendor product information, we designated the four-drawer filing cabinet for information separated into the following categories: products for the hair salon, relaxation and massage services, medi-spa treatments, and skin care services. The vendor information was organized alphabetically by product type within each drawer.

Now that you've had an opportunity to read about the various paper management systems, along with several client examples, I hope that you recognize that there isn't a one-size-fits-all system. Thank goodness for that, right? Instead, there are typically several systems you or your office will need to incorporate into your paper management workflow.

12 | Eliminate It—Paper to Recycle or Shred Now and in the Near Future

Technique #12: Get in the Habit of Eliminating Paper and Information Immediately If Not Needed or After the Purpose Has Been Served

Paper and information comes into your office every day from multiple locations: meetings, coworkers, your boss, and the mail, just to name a few. You can eliminate the papers from piling up by consciously making decisions about it as it arrives at your work area. However, without a good system to store and retrieve paper documents—coupled with a tendency to delay making decisions—you will most certainly end up with piles.

Following are two lists of paper that can be eliminated—some immediately, and others after the information contained on the document has served its purpose. These lists are intended to help you get a jump start on the amount of information or paperwork you may have accumulated over the years.

Some Examples of Paper You Can Eliminate Immediately

- Junk mail.
- Meeting agendas (especially if you have them stored electronically).
- Draft documents that you have stored electronically.
- Brochures for conferences that have taken place in the past that you did not attend.
- Outdated marketing materials (keep maybe just a copy or two for historical reasons).
- Invitations to events you know you won't attend.
- Journals and magazines more than a year old that you never read. There will always be more.
- Business newspapers more than three months old.
- Envelopes from the daily mail you've opened.
- Cash machine withdrawal receipts after you have recorded them.

Paper You Can Eliminate After the Purpose Has Been Served

- Documents distributed at meetings, especially if they are saved electronically.
- Any document that is a rough draft, a revision that is saved electronically, or a version of the document that is more current.
- Printed e-mail.
- Project notes or documentation from projects that never came to be, or from past projects that have been completed (especially when stored electronically).
- Articles or clippings you haven't read or reread in more than five years.
- Invitations to past events.
- Expired warranties and service contracts.
- Operation manuals for items you no longer own.
- Old catalogs (keep only the current one).
- Airline boarding passes that are more than a year old. You won't be able to claim mileage for a flight you've taken after a year.
- A travel itinerary for a completed trip.
- Expired coupons.

Paper You Can Eliminate After the Purpose Has Been Served—For Home-Based Businesses

- Utility bill statements after they have been paid. You don't need these for your taxes unless you deduct part of your home as a business expense. Don't keep these simply to compare how much your water bill was from one year to the next—because unless you've made an effort to do this in the past, chances are you won't do it in the future. If you do need a comparison at some point, you can call the company; they should be able to provide you with that information.
- Credit card statements that are more than a year old. Keep these only if you need to prove something for taxes, a major purchase, or capital improvement if you don't have the receipt.
- Canceled checks, unless they are needed for tax purposes.
- Investment and banking brochures you have never read.

- Expired insurance policies. Keep the declarations page, which states what your coverage is.

Be sure that you have two receptacles to sort paper into: one for recycling and one for shredding. There is no point in resorting these papers, so make the decision as you go and then follow through on removing the recycling and getting the papers shredded (if your office does not offer a shredding service).

Note: If you have any doubts about paperwork you must keep for financial, legal, or retention purposes, I recommend that you contact your attorney, tax professional, human resources department, or records retention specialist.

13 | Turning Piles into Files

Technique #13: Use the 10-Step Process to Turn Paper Piles into Files

Before you organize, revise, or implement any paper management system, it's helpful to understand why paper is such a challenge for most people. I've found in my experience that most people—no matter their job function or industry—face the following five major problems with organizing their paper and information:

1. Inability to locate documents needed in a timely fashion
2. Absence of a system, or lack of a system that works
3. Piles instead of files
4. Holding onto paper much longer than necessary
5. Difficulty determining how to categorize and label information for future retrieval

As discussed in a previous chapter, there are several types of paper management systems, each containing a different type of information.

The last section of this book is dedicated to the 10-step process I developed that works for the stuff in your office. It can also be used to help you organize your paperwork and go from piles to files. I know that some people have a strange affinity for their piles and even proclaim to me that they know where everything is. Yet it inevitably seems that they go to find something when I'm there that—surprise!—they aren't able to locate. Here's how you can use the 10 steps to help you eliminate the piles.

Step 1: Dedicate Time

Like any project or priority, what you don't make time for will not happen. For that reason, you need to schedule dedicated time for this project. You certainly don't need to tackle all of the paper in a day. You can start by asking yourself how long it took you to accumulate it.

Most likely, you'll be able to clear the surfaces in far less time. Do not set unrealistic expectations as to how long you expect this to take, or you may end up feeling frustrated and never complete the job. Paper is one of the more time-consuming things to organize; there are lots of decisions you'll need to make, and you can condense a lot into a small area. Here are a few ideas on how you may want to approach this project to keep the momentum going:

- **Tackle one pile per day.** Conduct a quick sort to determine if the material you encounter should go to the round file, shredder, or to be filed. Don't worry about what you will do with the paper you've kept. You will sort and begin to categorize during step 4.
- If your filing drawers are full of paper, **pull one file out per day** through which to sort. Keep only what you need, and then put the file back in the drawer. Remember, you are not creating your filing system yet; that comes later in the process.
- If you are storing paper in boxes and have multiple boxes to sort through and organize, **do just one box per day.**
- **Set aside 20 to 30 minutes a day,** several days a week, to work on a portion of your project. Pick a small task that you can complete in that amount of time so you feel as though you accomplished something.

Step 2: Gather Supplies

You won't need a lot of supplies to start this project, just some basics you probably already have in your office: recycling bin, shredder, garbage can, sticky notes, file folders, paper clips, stapler, and, of course, your papers.

Step 3: Establish a Staging Area

Have plenty of work surfaces to spread out your papers when you are working on this project, unless you enjoy working on the floor—which is actually something I don't recommend, because it may keep you from doing the majority of the work in the space where the papers will live.

Now you're ready to begin the next three steps.

Step 4: Sort

You will make decisions during this phase about the information you are keeping and begin to break it down or categorize it based on the system in which it will live. If you have a lot of papers to sort through, you may want to consider this a first pass and then fine-tune the categories for each system later. If, on the other hand, you already have your system in place and it just needs a few minor changes, you can approach this a bit differently, since there will be less sorting.

It's important that you have a vision and goal in mind for the paper and are aware of the kind of systems that you need to create. (You can refer to Chapter 11 for more information on various paper management systems and the type of information contained within them.) As you sort, you will begin to come up with categories for your system or systems. Steps 4, 5, and 6 can be accomplished at the same time when organizing paper.

As you look at each paper or individual file, you need to make a *decision* on whether you will keep it or eliminate it (step 5). If you are keeping it, set it aside; as you complete more sorting, you will begin to group like items together (step 6). This is the creation of categories. Don't try to perfect the process at this point, especially if you have a lot of paper to put in order. Instead, take a quick pass to see how much you can eliminate and then worry about finalizing your categories when you get to step 6.

It is no small undertaking to look at documents or files during the sorting phase to determine whether you need to keep them. It's an added—but necessary—task to then determine how to group these papers in a way that makes future filing and retrieval painless. Though it requires a lot of patience and commitment, you will find that it will be more than worth it in the long run.

Step 5: Eliminate

One of the most challenging aspects of creating and maintaining a paper management system is figuring out what to keep and deciding how long you should keep it. While you can use the previous chapter as an initial guideline for this, I would also recommend that you consult your company's record retention policy to determine *what* information should be kept and for how long. In the absence of a record retention schedule, you may want to consult with a CPA or an attorney. It might be a good idea to develop a policy—something that records and information management professionals can help you do. For more information, you can visit ARMA International at www.arma.org.

Step 6: Group Like Items Together

This step requires you to create all of your important paper management structure(s) or refine the systems you are currently using. I introduced four types of paper management systems in Chapter 11: daily action center, reference system, operational, and archival. Because everyone obviously has different paper management needs, it's close to impossible to provide examples of each system for various industries. So instead, I've opted to show the structure of an *Operational* system I created for a small business of about 150 employees as an example here. As you will read in Chapter 15, the system you create is more than just words on labels; it is the structure you define that is crucial to a well-organized, expandable, and maintained system.

I recommend that you group like items together when organizing your files; this will allow you to spend less time thinking about where they are stored when you need to retrieve the information. That is why it's important to go from *broad* to *specific* when grouping and labeling. For example, I created the following structure for my client in Washington State who had the following types of taxes to pay: 940, 941, Unemployment Insurance, Department of Labor & Industries, and Department of Revenue. If I simply placed each folder into the filing structure individually, it would be much more time consuming to locate each than it would be to find the section labeled **Taxes**.

By grouping all of the tax files together, it just takes a second to find them.

Following is a partial outline of their operational system with the subfiles included in each section. *Note:* Each section is designated by boldface type, and the subfiles are listed beneath the section.

Advertising
Google Ads
Magazines
Newspapers
Yellow Pages

Checking Account
B of A–9876
Chase–0123
Chase–4567

Contracts—Client
No subfiles used; rather filed by date—most current in front

Contracts—Operational
No subfiles used; rather filed by date—most current in front

Employees
Filed by last name first, first name last

Insurance
Dental
Liability
Medical
Vehicle

Legal

Licenses
Business License

Marketing
Marketing Materials—Finals

Merchant Services
American Express
Intuit Payment Solutions

Phones
Cell
VoIP

Printing
    Filed by company name that completed the specific project

Public Relations

Receipts
    Filed by month

Reseller Permit

Statements
Comcast
Idearc
Sprint
Staples
Verizon

Taxes
940
941
Department of Labor & Industries
Department of Revenue
Unemployment Insurance

Trademark
Trademarks—Filed
Trademarks—Pending

Website

Although you may already have paper management systems in place, you might consider tweaking or recategorizing them if you've found that it's more challenging than you like to admit to find information when needed. This will also give you an opportunity to eliminate previously filed information that you know you do not need to keep.

Step 7: Examine Your Space

Before you go shopping, take a moment to reexamine the amount of space you have to store documents in your office. Will you be able to store them all where you work? Will some be moved to another location in the office? Will some go to archives? Does certain information need to be locked up? Do the files need to be portable? It's important to know what the volume is and what amount of space you have in which to store them before you purchase furniture or other equipment to contain them. Take measurements now, so that you have them when you're ready to make a purchase.

Step 8: Shop

The key with shopping is to not waste your time purchasing a product that doesn't fit or serve the intended purpose. This won't be an issue if you've followed the steps in order thus far. The problem so often encountered during this step is that most people want to shop first and purchase something that they think will somehow *solve* the problem. In reality, it may not be solving the problem, but instead only adding to it.

I have found, however, that there is sometimes an exception to purchasing a few products in advance—like file folders or hanging files—when organizing your files. Though it's pretty difficult to do this project without folders, you may already have a supply in the office. If you desire to set up your system using particular colors, types of files, and specific labels, you can purchase them at the start, knowing you may run out of a certain color or type and need to purchase more later on. Or you can wait until you come to this step and see how you want to use various colors to help you identify certain information or systems. Either way, I recommend consistency in the products you use. Always make sure you have extra on hand to add on to the system; otherwise, you'll end up grabbing what is available—something that could eventually lead to having a file system that no longer looks consistent.

Step 9: Install Product

There won't be a lot of product to install when organizing files; you'll typically use equipment you already have to house them and might just need a few new cabinets or filing carts. Of course, if you decided to standardize on a particular type or color of file, you may end up swapping the folders at this point (if you hadn't purchased them at the beginning of the project). If you take the advice I offer in Chapter 15 about labeling your files, you may end up labeling during this step—which can sometimes be the more time-consuming process than getting new equipment into place.

Step 10: Maintain

Paper is a system that requires regular maintenance, which for some may mean daily maintenance. You will need to determine how much time this will take you and how often it must occur. I can't stress enough what an important step this is, and that it is *much* easier to stay on top of on a regular basis than to let it pile up.

Tips
1. There is no right or wrong way to create a paper management system. If you establish a structure that works for you and/or others in your office, you will be more likely to use it than if you simply copy something someone else created.
2. If you don't like to file information immediately, have a "to be filed" location or basket for these documents—which should not require any more action than to be filed if placed in this area. Then if you need a document and it's not filed, you only have to check for it in one other place.

3. *Immediately* toss or shred paper that you do not need.
4. Use straight-line filing by placing filing tabs on hanging file folders in the same location, such as the left side. When you stagger the tabs and then have to add or remove a tab, it messes up the placement of the existing tabs. Putting the tabs in a straight line eliminates the need to reposition labels. Since we read left to right, I tend to put the tabs on the left. If this doesn't work because you can't see the labels from where you sit at your desk or stand to look in a drawer, put them on the right. Whatever you do, keep it consistent.
5. Leave at least six inches of space in each filing drawer or shelf so that you can easily find what you are looking for and add additional documents or files.
6. Place the most current papers in the front when filing. That way, if you need to refer back to something that happened recently, it will be in chronological order.
7. Avoid using too many colors in your filing system. You will run out of colors before you run out of categories.
8. If you are creating your system from scratch, do all labeling *last* so that you are sure you have the file folders and hanging files labeled exactly how you want them—and do not have to waste time relabeling later.
9. Create a file folder or envelope for any contact information you run across such as addresses, phone numbers, e-mail addresses, and business cards. This way, you can keep this information together as you are sorting through your files. You can then create a system to store this information later in the process.
10. Edit your files annually, if not twice a year. At a minimum, you should go through your files on a yearly basis and eliminate what is no longer needed or move it to archives.
11. Establish a location for reading materials, such as magazines, newspapers, and other documents you want to read. Magazines and newspapers should go in one location and your other reading material—such as newsletter or things you print off the Internet—should be placed in another location, such as a folder that you can grab and take with you to catch up on your reading.

14 | Implementing the PAPERS™ Method

Technique #14: Use the PAPERS Method Daily

The PAPERS method will help you process and make decisions about any paper you touch, every single day. Whether it's office paperwork or the mail, this system will help you take control of document flow and eliminate the paper chaos.

How the PAPERS Method Works

P: The first *P* stands for **Process**. You must process all paperwork—which requires at least one if not more of the following steps.

You've probably heard the saying, "only touch a piece of paper once." I don't agree with this advice.

Any piece of paper you have requires making a choice about the information contained on it. The first step involves making a decision about the information. This may be that you can't do anything further with it at the time, so you need a place to temporarily store the material until a later date. Keep in mind that the nearest horizontal surface is not that temporary place. An excellent location for a temporary storage place may be in your daily action center, as discussed in Chapter 11.

A: The *A* stands for **Action**. Can you act on the information immediately, or do you need to defer action to later? If so, you will need to store it in a temporary location until you have time to take action. You'll want to make sure that the location is close by and not in an out-of-the-way area, or you run the risk of forgetting about it.

P: The second *P* stands for **Pass it on**. Don't hesitate to forward the information to someone who's responsible for taking action on it.

E: The *E* stands for **Eliminate it**; in other words, either shred it or recycle it. Don't hold onto information—whether paper or electronic—that you won't make time to file somewhere that provides easy retrieval in the future.

R: Information will cross your desk or your mailbox that you'll want to **Read**. Unfortunately, you will not always have time to read it immediately. Until you have the chance to read it, you need a location where it can temporarily live.

S: Once you have processed the papers and information you've received and realized that you don't need to Eliminate it, Read it, Act on it, or Pass it on, then chances are that you need to **Store** it. The primary reasons you would want to store it are for financial or legal reasons, or you may choose to do so because it is either reference information or memorabilia.

The **PAPERS** method is one that I've been using with our clients for years. To organize anything, you must have a process to ensure follow-through and completion; that is why the first *P* stands for Process.

Whatever process you use—whether it's my PAPERS method or another—you need a system to stay on top of the daily deluge of information you receive. Failing to have a process in place—and use it—is the main cause of paper disorganization.

Once you've had an opportunity to create some of the systems presented in other chapters, give the PAPERS method a try. Between the combination of having a place to put the information and a process for sorting through it and making decisions, you will be well on your way to reducing the amount of paper piled up on a daily basis.

15 | More Than Just a Label

Technique #15: Design the Paper Management Structure First, and Then Create the Labels

Words on labels are just that: words. If your goal is to create a paper management system, your labels are going to play a bigger role than you may have previously considered. You need to think of your labels in terms of the filing structure or paper management system you are designing.

Design the System First, Then Label

While the act of making a label is quite simple, knowing what information to put on the label is the challenging part. Why? Because you're doing more than merely placing your papers into folders and dropping them into a filing cabinet. You are creating a system to which you can add additional information and retrieve material when needed. Haphazardly putting labels on files without looking at the bigger picture will result in information that you will either forget you had or won't be able to find when needed.

If you're creating a system from scratch because you either (1) didn't have one to begin with or (2) are fed up with your existing system, do yourself a favor: Put temporary labels on your files until you're done. Making labels as you go or before you've designed the entire system will waste both time and products. It is far more efficient to sit down and make the labels at one time. I see this kind of wasted time and material frequently; people are so eager to get this task done that they can't wait until the system is finalized to do the labeling. However, waiting pays off substantially in the long run.

Temporary Labels

To temporarily label file folders or hanging files, use sticky notes. Simply place the sticky side on the top edge of the file folder tab, and

123

then write the label name on the sticky note. For hanging files, turn the sticky note upside down, and write the label name on the bottom of the sticky note. Place the sticky note on the hanging file so that the writing is sticking up just over the top edge of the hanging file. This way, if you don't have enough time to complete your system at one time, you can place the hanging files in the drawer and be able to see your temporary labels and retrieve the necessary information.

Words or a System?

When deciding on how to label your files, you want to ensure that you are choosing meaningful words that will help create your system.

Labeling Products for File Folders

You can label your folders using the following products:

1. Hand–held labeling machine.
2. Computer-generated file folder labels.
3. Viewables file folder labels.
4. Erasable file labels.
5. Or you don't have to use any product; instead, just write on the file folder directly.

Hand–Held Labeling Machine

Here are a few tips about labeling files with a hand-held labeler:

1. Choose a standard font style, size, and label tape color for consistency.
2. If you have multiple labels to create, make them all at once to save label tape. Enter your label, press the space bar three or four times, enter your next label, then enter another three or four spaces, and so on, until the memory is full and you must print the labels. Once printed, use scissors to cut the labels. Printing each label separately would result in a lot of excess, unusable tape on either end of the label.

Computer-Generated File Folder Labels

There are a couple of ways you can create file folder labels on your computer, both of which require you to use templates. Avery (www.avery.com) has hundreds of label templates on their website. It doesn't matter if you're using a PC or a Mac; there are labels for each operating system. You can download the templates and save to your computer.

I am a PC user; I typically use the label templates that can be found in Microsoft Word. You can access the labels in the following way.

From the Mailings ribbon bar, select Labels. The Envelopes and Labels dialog box will open, and you select the tab called Labels. Clicking on the Options button will give you the ability to select a label vendor, such as Avery or Office Depot. Depending on your selection of a vendor, you will see many product numbers to select from. Notice that once you select a label, it will display information such as label type, height, width, and page size. So, for example, Avery label #5666 is the file folder label template. If you purchased Avery labels at the store, the #5666 on the package corresponds to the label number in Microsoft Word. Many of the office retail stores carry their own version of labels, and even though the label sizes are the same, the product number is different. Make sure the labels are the same size before you create and print a sheet of them.

Once it's made, save your label template so you don't have to re-create it each time you need to print labels. If you print labels often, place a shortcut to the label file on your desktop. If you consistently archive the same documents or folders each year, create a sheet of labels for these files, and each year you will have minor modifications to make before you print a new batch of labels. This will also serve as a guide for the files to archive.

Tips to Ensure Your Labels Turn Out as Planned and Look Good, Too
1. Pick a font you like, and use it consistently.
2. There's no reason you can't print the labels in color if you like a particular shade.
3. Use a font size of 14 or 16. This will allow you to easily identify the folder but not be so large that the label won't fit on one line.
4. Before you print the labels, print a test page on paper and hold it behind the sheet of labels to verify printing placement.

5. If you're printing the labels on a laser printer, run that sheet of labels through the printer only two or three times. Any more than that and you will start to see your labels turn slightly gray, since the toner leaves a film each time it goes through. (You won't have this problem if you're using an ink jet printer.)

Viewables File Folder Labels

The Viewables Labeling system by Smead is one of my favorite labeling products. You can make labels for both file folders and hanging files with this product.

After purchasing the Viewables software, you'll need to purchase Viewables product #64915, a package of 160 file folder labels that are specially sized to wrap around the file folder tab. The software allows you to customize the color of the label's top; each label holds up to three rows of text. You can also decide if you want to put a clear label protector over the top to keep it from being marked up or mangled.

Erasable File Labels

If you like how labels look on your files but hate the thought of having to relabel folders as the contents change—or placing one label on top of another—you may want to consider using erasable file folder labels. These labels can be written on with a Sharpie and erased as needed.

Write Directly on the Folder

If you feel that labeling your files using one of the previously mentioned methods is more trouble than it's worth, there's no reason you can't write directly on the folder. Creating and maintaining this system is all about personal preference; after all, it's *your* system that you get to look at every day. However, if you share these files with others, I would definitely recommend using some kind of labeling product.

Labeling Products for Hanging Files

You can label your hanging files using the following products.

Plastic tabs that come with the box of hanging files

Each box of hanging files comes with a set of plastic tabs and inserts you can use to label the hanging files. Since I write big, I find it hard to fit my category on the little paper insert that goes inside the tab. Avery #8167 labels, which are 0.5 inches high by 1.7 inches wide, solve this problem. They allow you to type your labels on the computer and then print them on the paper inserts.

Viewables Hanging File Tabs

Viewables are my favorite product to use with hanging file folders. Whenever I show this to someone, they always think it's one of the coolest filing products they've seen. While they will certainly take you some extra time and require a small investment, I've found it to be more than worth it—considering how easy they make filing and retrieving information.

What I also like about this product is that the program remembers which labels you've used on the sheet, and when you're ready to print more, it will automatically pick up where you left off—even without having to save your work. After you've printed the labels, placed them over the three-dimensional plastic tab, and covered them with the clear protector, you insert the plastic tabs into the slots in the hanging file—just like the plastic tabs that come with a box of hanging folders.

A Few Tips That Will Help You with Your Viewables

1. Decide whether you want to print the labels in color. If you choose to do so, use the colors to identify different sections or types of filing. Even though you can make your own custom colors, I still like black and white, since it's usually the easiest to read.

2. You can print up to three lines of text on the front side of the label. The top view of the label will be the same as the top row of the text on the front side.

3. Be sure to align the printer when printing Viewables the first time—and if you change printers, align the replacement printer as well. The software will always detect if you haven't aligned

the printers; don't skip over this step, or the labels may not print properly.

4. After aligning the printer, print a test copy on a sheet of paper. Hold the sheet of paper behind the label to ensure the printing lines up. If all looks good, you're ready to print directly on the labels. Once you're ready to print, simply put a check next to each label you wish to print. You can also select "mark for printing" and then "all labels" from the Label menu. While this involves an extra step, I think it's worth it to be 100 percent certain that you print your labels correctly the first time.

5. When you're done printing, you don't need to save what you've just printed (unless, of course, you want to print those labels again). When the program asks if you want to save, select no; the software will automatically remember which labels you've printed.

6. If you're printing on an ink jet printer, be sure you let the labels dry before placing them on the plastic tabs; otherwise, you'll smear the ink and waste labels. Since you get 32 labels and 25 plastic tabs in one package, you do have seven extra labels in case one or two get messed up or need to be changed in the future.

7. Although I've had a lot of practice putting labels and label protectors on the tabs after creating several thousand, I will admit that the first few are the biggest challenge—until you determine your preferred method. Let me share what works best for me. The part of the label that contains the strip of color (or black) is the first part you want to affix to the plastic tab. The label is not designed to touch each end, so I just line up the strip of color close to either end of the plastic tab and fold the sides over. Notice before placing the label on the tab that one side is very narrow, and the other is quite a bit wider. You want to ensure that you have your label facing the correct way before you fold the sides over. Once the label's on, the tricky part comes next: affixing the clear label protector without wrinkles or lifting ink off the label in the process. I usually lay the tab down with the wide side facing up. Then, using two hands, I am able to take the label protector, place it squarely over the bottom edge of the plastic tab, and fold over the other side.

Reading about how to make these labels may sound like a lot of work, but trust me—it's a small amount of extra work that's more than worth the effort. I'm sure you can see now why I always recommend that you *temporarily* label your files to save time down the road.

Erasable Hanging Tabs

Just like the erasable file folder labels, there's a similar product available for hanging files. You can use a Sharpie to write on and erase the labels as needed. This very simple and quick solution may be a perfect option for you if you don't want to spend the extra time or expense creating the Viewables or if you just don't like the looks of the plastic tabs that come with the box of hanging files.

Use Nothing

A final option may be to use nothing at all to label your hanging files. While I don't typically recommend this as a solution, it's your filing system, not mine. In the past, I have used the Viewables tabs on some hanging files to group a section together. Then I've left several of the hanging files without any tab because they are part of the group, and it wasn't necessary to put a tab on each folder.

As you can see, there are several labeling options. Consider your options and the upkeep that's necessary as you select one, as well as how each system you design will benefit from the label type you choose. A nicely labeled system will make it easier and faster to file, since it allows you to quickly locate the information you need. After you create and label your systems, they become much more than a filing or paper management classification. They are the retrieval system that will allow you to quickly locate what you are looking for and make it less likely that you'll create a duplicate file for something you could not find.

III Electronic Information Management

16 | Manage Information Overload

Technique #16: Develop and Implement Strategies to Help Alter Behavior and Habits That Will Reduce Your Feeling of Information Overload

I'm sure I don't need to tell you that nowadays, more so than ever, information comes at you from multiple directions all day long. You feel like an out-of-breath hamster that doesn't know how to stop the wheel from turning so fast. Chances are that you're not done with your work when you leave the office at the end of the day—because you are still returning phone calls and answering e-mail. While I believe everyone is aware of this, many company cultures force people to make compromises. Solopreneurs and entrepreneurs may find themselves in a slightly different situation—one where they must do something on a weekend or evening. However, because you are the boss in this scenario, you can take time off when needed. It's easier for you to take whatever free time for yourself is necessary during the work week to compensate for the time you spend working on evenings and weekends.

I don't think anyone will ever be able to come up with the *perfect* way to stop feeling information overload; however, there are techniques you can use to alter your behavior and habits to make the workday a bit less chaotic. Some of these behaviors involve setting boundaries, turning off the background distractions, and reestablishing expectations. I recently had a conversation with a marketing executive who lamented about all of the electronic pollution and useless e-mail he receives daily. He complained that the people at his office don't understand the proper usage of the "To," "CC," and "BCC" fields and that everyone copied everyone else to make sure they've covered their you-know-whats. Another example: A client of mine who is also a friend responded to one of my e-mails while she was on vacation, stating that "my boss said I could disconnect on my vacation"—but as you can see, she was still on e-mail while she was away. I know that she was responding to my e-mail, as a friend and not as a client, but I had to laugh when I read that. After all, she was on vacation—shouldn't she have been able to rest and recharge her batteries?

135

Some Techniques for Dealing with Information Overload or Electronic Chaos

1. **Technology devices that have an on switch also have an off switch.** Try using it once in awhile. Set a time each evening when you will no longer check e-mail on your computer or mobile device, and on weekends allow yourself to check only during certain times that you establish.

2. **Set boundaries.** If you make yourself available 24 hours a day/7 days a week, people will expect an immediate response from you all the time. When they can't reach you via e-mail, they may call all of the numbers they have for you. It's very difficult to reset these parameters once you've set unrealistic boundaries.

3. **Unsubscribe.** Don't be afraid to unsubscribe from something—an e-mail list, newsletter, or membership—if your needs have changed, or if you automatically hit the delete key without opening it every time it appears in your inbox.

4. **Create rules in your inbox to eliminate distractions.** E-mail of an informational nature, such as newsletters, airline and hotel offers, and list serves, can be moved immediately from the inbox to folders to view at a later date. This helps to free your inbox for e-mail that requires more immediate attention and action. An explanation and example of how to create a rule is provided in Chapter 18.

5. **Shut off automatic alerts.** If it's not a critical component of your job function to respond to FaceBook posts or see every tweet the minute it's sent, then disable these instant alerts so that you're better able to focus on the task at hand.

6. **Turn off the e-mail pop-up box** that tells you that you have new e-mail. Every time this shows up in the corner of your screen, you are distracted from what you're doing, so do your best to eliminate this distraction, and check your e-mail periodically during the day.

7. **Use your Out of Office e-mail response on evenings and weekends.** This will let your contacts know that you aren't available during these personal blocks of time.

8. **Update your voicemail to reflect when you are available to return calls.** This will let callers know when they can

expect to hear back from you—which will hopefully keep them from constantly calling. Just make sure you stick to your word.

9. **Eliminate spam.** Our business systems consultant, Robert Strasser, calculated that each spam message costs 2.5 cents—including the bandwidth it occupies, hard drive space, and end user cost to delete. He recommends Postini™ Services from Google to do away with these messages.

10. **Be disciplined.** Adhere to the rules you create for yourself.

11. **Set expectations.** Establish expectations with others that set you up for success so that someone doesn't give you something to do at the last minute and expect an instant turnaround.

12. **Reset expectations.** You will never be able to get off the hamster wheel if you don't evaluate and reestablish your expectations from time to time. You must acknowledge behavior and make changes that are appropriate for you.

13. **Don't feel pressured into an unrealistic deadline.** Take the discussion off-line to establish a more realistic one.

14. **Shift from being *reactive* to being *proactive*.** Understand how you are spending your time in regard to information coming at you from many directions. Are you a firefighter, tackling the issues as they arise, or are you on top of things? You can make the shift from the former to the latter by implementing the techniques in this book.

15. **Be honest with yourself.** Which unproductive or nonessential considerations work against your core job function? Which of these steps might you be able to implement to help eliminate some of your information overload?

Resetting Expectations: The Taxi Accident Example

When the editor at Wiley first approached me about writing this book, I had to give serious consideration to my previous commitments and the short time frame in which I'd have to write it—since I knew the first half of 2010 was booked. I concluded that I would be able to complete the project in three months; I would plan the rest of my activities, clients, and speaking engagements around it and still have the manuscript delivered before the September 30, 2010, due date. What I *didn't* plan for was the accident I was in on June 25, when the taxi I was in on a business trip rear-ended the car in front of me. As a result, I wound up with a sprained left wrist and soft tissue damage to several parts of my back.

Needless to say, it was a bit challenging to type one handed, much less sit for more than about an hour at a time and focus when I was in constant pain. I really didn't know how I was going to make my deadline; I had taken most of the month of July off to write and instead spent nearly five days a week seeing doctors and specialists and got very little writing done. In mid-July, I had an honest conversation with my editor and made her aware of my predicament. While I'm a very goal-oriented person who feels that it's important to honor deadlines, I was a bit nervous about the looming September 30 date. After a brief conversation about the publishing schedule, my editor was able to grant me an additional half-month to complete the book. Now, I am no longer stressed or overwhelmed with the deadline, and I know I will do an even better job of writing an exceptional manuscript. I took my own advice to reset expectations when necessary. (It probably helped a bit that I didn't ask for an extension on September 25 either!)

It would be unrealistic to claim that the *information overload* you experience will ever go away. Instead, you need to learn how to manage it—just as you need to manage your time. While you may not be able (or even want) to completely change your corporate culture, you can start reducing the overload by practicing the techniques in this chapter and helping to get others in your organization on board. At the very least, these techniques will help you become more productive, remain focused, and eliminate unnecessary distractions. Solopreneurs are in a much better position to control the overload or make changes.

Let's face it; almost everyone is overwhelmed from time to time—maybe even on a daily basis—by all of the information we encounter in the form of e-mail, voicemail, texts, tweets, list serves, newsletters, and more. And you most likely receive all of this in addition to the work that's already on your plate. You need to start by determining what is necessary versus what is a distraction. While you might have to reset expectations, I would not suggest walking into your boss's office until you know exactly how you're spending your time. Tracking your daily activities for a two- to three-week period may be just the eye-opener that you need. You will be in a much better position to renegotiate once you understand the true cause of your information overload.

Remember—only *you* can make a conscious choice as to how much time you will stay connected and how quickly you can feasibly respond.

17 | Using Naming Conventions and Version Control on Your Computer Files

Technique #17: Implement File Naming Convention Best Practices

Technique #18: Implement Version Control for Your Electronic Documents

"Naming conventions" and "version control" are two phrases I mention to clients during seminars that receive a lot of questions pertaining to meaning. This comes as no surprise to me, since the majority of our clients do not practice these techniques. However, once we start explaining this easy-to-implement practice, they quickly realize what makes it so valuable and how it will increase productivity.

The two primary reasons to consider adopting these techniques is that they will allow you and your coworkers to spend less time looking for files and eliminate the need to re-create a document because you couldn't locate it. These issues cost companies a lot of money each year in lost time.

File Naming Convention Best Practices

1. **Give your document a descriptive file name.** The name of the file should tell you what it contains, so specifically that you don't need to open it to uncover its contents. Descriptive file names will be easier to locate via search utilities for documents on your computer or shared drives. I provide some examples later in the chapter.

2. **Start general, and move to the specifics.** Using more general or broader terms at the beginning of the file name (like the particular project or event) and putting the more detailed description at the end (such as the date the file was created, the version, or the initials of the individual who created it) will quickly narrow down your search.

3. **Start with "File Save As."** If you plan to modify an existing document, the first thing you need to do is a "File Save As" so that you can be assured you don't accidentally overwrite the

existing version. You may want to include a date or document version as part of this name (see best practices 6 and 7).

4. **Don't use extraneous characters.** Limit special characters to a dash, underscore, or dot. Do not use any of the following in file or directory names: " * : < >? \/ |.

5. **Keep extra spaces to a minimum.** Limit total combined directory and file name to 255 characters.

6. **Include a date.** Use a date as part of the file name to show when the document was created or revised. Don't rely on the Save As date or created date to provide you with this information.

7. **Use document versions.** Implement a version control system to show the latest version of the document.

8. **Use initials.** Implement a policy to include the initials of the individual or department that created or modified the document. For example, a file name with the initials of *hrrs* at the end of it stands for Human Resources Robert Strasser. Or you could just include the initials of *hr* or *rs* at the end.

Bad File Name Examples

The following file names are too general; neither you nor your coworkers will be able to tell what is contained within them.

Doc1 (Hmmm . . . I have no idea what's in this document.)

June 14 (What did you do this day? A date tells you nothing.)

Presentation (What presentation was it, and what group was it for?)

Seminar Handout (What seminar is this handout for?)

Policies and Procedures (Somewhat better, but I still don't know what the policies and procedure are *for*.)

Descriptive File Name Examples

Proposal to Install Exchange Server - WIS 6.14.11 R2 (This file name tells you that it's a proposal for a specific piece of business, the date it was originally written, and that it's the second revision.)

Outlook 2010 Presentation to Coca Cola 4.15.11 V2 (Now you know which potential client the presentation was made to, along with the date and version of the presentation.)

Relocation Policies and Procedures 3.23.11 (This is more descriptive as it tells you *what* the policies and procedures are for and provides a date of creation.)

Version Control

Using version or revision numbers on your documents will help you and others distinguish which document is the most current. If you are working on a document with others, it is a good idea to save the file with the next version or revision number *before* you start making changes; this way, you have the previous version should you need to refer back to it. You can use a *V* or *Ver* for the version number in the document or an *R* or *Rev* for the revision number. There is really no difference here; both have the same meaning, and it's simply a matter of personal preference. However, I do recommend that you standardize on one or the other. Even though you can use tracking features in documents or file system versioning control, I would not advise relying solely on this method.

Making a Document Read-Only

If you have a Word document or a PowerPoint presentation that you want to ensure remains as the master, you can change the properties to read-only. This is a great way to make sure that someone doesn't inadvertently click "Save" instead of "File Save As."

Follow These Steps
1. Right-click on the name of the document.
2. Select **Properties** from the submenu.
3. Click in the **Read-Only** box.
4. Click **OK**.

When you need to use the master in the future, simply open it and save a copy with the new file name. This way you ensure that your master is never changed.

You don't need to wait until you have time to rename your documents before implementing this system. Start today, and continue to do so moving forward. It's important to put a plan in place that provides guidelines and expectations as to how you name files and handle versions—and then start using it immediately. You can go back and rename files as needed at a later date; in fact, in doing so, you may find some that are no longer needed. The key to an effective naming convention and version control technique is that you have *consistency*. There isn't a right or wrong way to implement this, except for the lack of company guidelines that state how your organization will accomplish this technique.

18 | How to Take Control of E-Mail and Implement a System for Tracking and Organization

Technique #19: Implement Strategies to Help You Control E-Mail, Implement a System to Keep Track of It All, and Eliminate the Vast Quantity of Messages in Your Inbox

E-mail—the once-novel idea that has become the beast that buries so many of us on a daily basis. The people I advise often ask me how to take control of e-mail, devise a system to keep track of it all, and eliminate the vast quantity of messages in the inbox. In this chapter, I will provide you with several simple and quick-to-implement techniques. While these methods may not take your inbox down to zero items—a goal I find to be unrealistic for most—they *will* help you stay on top of e-mail daily, implement a solid follow-up process, and assist with organizing, filing, and retrieving e-mails that you need to keep.

You can implement many of these techniques using the e-mail program of your choice. However, the topics for which I've provided specific steps have been documented using Microsoft Outlook 2010.

Maybe you've heard it said, "Never check e-mail in the morning." I don't agree with this proposition. While it may work for some, it does not for most. Why? Because many people's jobs require them to spend a good portion of their day on e-mail. I also do not subscribe to the theory that you should check e-mail only two or three times a day. Only you can determine how often you should check, based on your job function. However, I've found that the following guidelines do help—regardless of your particular position or the frequency with which you need to check your e-mail:

Two-Minute Rule. I use the following two-minute rule with my clients: If you need to be in your inbox for a significant part of the day, answer e-mails that will take two minutes or less to get them out of your inbox.

Acknowledge E-Mail. If you request information from someone, be courteous and acknowledge the receipt of the e-mail with a simple thanks to let them know that you got it. The sender doesn't have a crystal ball to know if you received the e-mail, let alone took the time to read it. If you receive an e-mail that is going to require a bit of time before you can respond, be polite and let the sender know that you will get back to them with a response—and provide a time frame if you know it. In today's fast-paced work environment, people have come to expect quick responses. They may begin to wonder if you are taking action if you don't answer and clarify when they can expect to hear from you again.

Organize the Subject Matter of Your E-Mail

No one likes to read an e-mail with long paragraphs that go on and on and on. When you compose and send an e-mail like this, the reader is likely to close it and never bother to respond. Instead, compose your e-mail using short sentences, bullet points, and numbered lists. If you need to draw attention to a specific item that requires immediate attention or a response, use the bold or underline features or consider using a different color of font for the few words or sentence that you need to highlight. This will help draw the reader's eye to that part of the message, so nothing is overlooked.

Processing E-Mail

Several years ago, I asked one of my clients why she had 14,000 e-mails in her inbox. She told me she didn't know how to delete them. And she was serious. In fact, many of my clients leave all their e-mail in their inbox. Some, like her, have saved more than 10,000. That is *a lot* of e-mail. And while your computer may not appear cluttered from the outside, this kind of backup can trigger a digital disaster. E-mails and files are the main source of the mess; since storage space is so inexpensive, it's easy to keep everything. However, just as it is with physical clutter, it's important to create and maintain a digital organizing system. And what may work for one person may not work for the next. You must decide what's best for you.

Many companies limit the size of employees' inboxes, forcing them to periodically clean it out. If you aren't sure whether your company has these restrictions in place—or what they are—check with your Information Systems department.

Don't be seduced by the promise of unlimited space. Instead, keep in mind that it's not about the amount of space you have to work with, but rather the system you develop to stay on top of things that will allow you to retrieve information when you need it. It helps if you think of your e-mail inbox as you do an inbox for paper. If you take the same actions you would with paper, it will go a long way toward organizing your e-mail.

The following is a simple, four-step system you can implement that will help you create and maintain e-mail organization.

> **Delete It.** Once you've read the e-mail and you realize you don't need this information, delete it—*now*. Otherwise, you will have to open it again later, make another decision (or the same one again), and take action. If you have multiple e-mails on the same subject, delete all but the most recent and decide whether you need to file it for future use.
>
> **Delegate It.** If an e-mail requires someone else to take action, forward it to the appropriate person. Then usually you can delete it. If you need to save a copy, you can retrieve a copy from your Sent Items file or move it to a designated folder when forwarding or replying to the e-mail. Using the **Save Sent Item To** option in Outlook allows you to save the e-mail you are replying to or forwarding directly to one of your subfolders. After you have pressed the **Reply** or **Forward** button, select the **Options** tab and then you will see the **Save Sent Item To** button (Figure 18.1). Click on this to select the folder where you want the e-mail to be stored, rather than the default (which is your **Sent** file).

**Save Sent
Item To ▾**

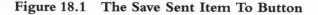

Figure 18.1　The Save Sent Item To Button

File It. If an e-mail contains information you may need in the future but does not require any immediate action, put it in a subfolder—based on a particular project, person, or activity—so you can retrieve it later. This is the most difficult part in creating an e-mail system for many people, because they don't know what to label the folders. It's fairly simple to create and label a new folder; however, establishing a framework so that you can retrieve the information easily in the future can be difficult.

Take Action. You take action on e-mails that require a response. There are two types of e-mail that fall into this category: those to which you can reply in 2 minutes or less (see the previous 2-Minute Rule) and those that require more time for consideration, project work, or research. Decide after responding whether you will delete or file the e-mail.

From the standpoint of personal productivity—and the ability to retrieve information later—using these four actions will help you begin to create an organized e-mail system. However, as with any system you create, getting started is paramount—and regular maintenance is vital. You don't need to wait until your e-mail inbox is cleared out before implementing the four actions. Instead, start today with the e-mails you receive and apply these actions to older e-mails over time.

Make Time to Manage E-Mail

Everyone needs a process for managing e-mail; I've shared one with you that I know works. However, whatever process you select, you need to put time and effort into it on a daily basis—which means you need to *make* the time to manage e-mail. When you don't, it piles up in your inbox, and you run the risk of overlooking something with a deadline. And the more information you have, the more time you will spend looking for something when you need it.

Write a Descriptive Subject Line

Subject lines should tell e-mail recipients what the e-mail is about, without them even opening it. A descriptive subject line also helps in the future when someone is searching for an e-mail using key words. A good rule when composing the subject line is to go from *broad* to *specific*.

Examples:
Advertising Information for 6.20.11 Deadline
Follow Up from NSA Conference—Information You Requested
Sometimes it is helpful to include a date in the subject line when the message contains date-specific information. However, if the e-mail has no relevance to a date, don't worry about including one.

Use Acronyms in the Subject Line

Sometimes you need to send a one-line e-mail to someone. Why bother writing a descriptive subject line and then restating it in the body of your e-mail? By using the following acronyms at the beginning or end of your subject line, you are telling the reader the following:

EOM = End of Message. In other words, your e-mail's recipient does not need to open the message to read your entire message—unless they intend to respond.

NRN = No Response Necessary. You have clearly stated in your subject line that you are not expecting a response; the e-mail is for information purposes only.

RN = Response Needed.

AR = Action Required.

If you get into the habit of using these acronyms—or others that your organization or department standardizes on—everyone will understand the use, thus making e-mail processing more efficient.

Examples of Subject Lines That Use One of These Acronyms

Confirming Our Meeting Today at 2pm in the Conference Room—EOM

Please Call Me When You Get In Today—EOM

HWS Meeting Minutes from 3.8.11—NRN

Auction Committee Report 2.10.11—NRN

Compose the Subject Line after Writing the E-Mail

Composing the e-mail first and then writing the subject line allows you the opportunity to determine what single message you are conveying. Then you can summarize it succinctly in the subject line and let the reader know exactly what topic you need to cover.

Change the Subject Line When It Makes No Sense

If the e-mail's subject has changed, alter the subject line to match. When possible, avoid multiple subjects in one e-mail; the e-mail thread will be too complicated to follow. Instead, begin a new e-mail for the new subject.

Change the Subject Line for E-Mails That You File for Future Reference

A descriptive subject line that jogs your memory will help you quickly retrieve information in the future that you store in your inbox sub-folders. To change a subject line, take the following steps.

1. Move the e-mail to its destination, and open it.
2. Select the text in the "Subject line" and delete it.
3. Type your new, more descriptive subject line.
4. Save and close the e-mail.

Dragging an E-Mail Address between the To, Cc, and Bcc Fields

Click on the e-mail address and drag it to the appropriate field—To, Cc, or Bcc—depending on each recipient's role in the e-mail. You expect a response from those in the To field and are simply providing information as an FYI only to those in the Cc field. This helps recipients understand what you expect from them. Don't send the e-mail off in such a rush that you don't make the time to verify the addresses in all fields. You may even find that you can delete some e-mail addresses for people who don't need a copy of your response.

Eliminate E-Mail Address That Display in the To, Cc, and Bcc Fields

Individuals to whom you've sent e-mail in the past will have their e-mail addresses displayed in the To, Cc, or Bcc fields. You'll see these addresses pop up in the scroll box as you start typing (Figure 18.2). There will probably come a time when you'll want to eliminate one of these addresses because it is no longer correct, used, or someone you plan to e-mail in the future. Here's how to eliminate an e-mail address; the process is the same whether you are in the To, Cc, or Bcc fields.

1. In the **To** field, start typing the name of the e-mail recipient. You will begin to see a list of e-mail addresses that you've used in the past.
2. Mouse over the e-mail address you desire to eliminate, and you will see an X next to the e-mail address that you are hovering over.
3. Click on the X to remove that e-mail address.

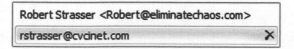

Figure 18.2 Eliminating an E-Mail Address

Note: This does not delete the e-mail address from any of the address books. Rather, it just removes it from your computer's cache.

Marking E-Mail as Read or Unread

After you read an e-mail, it no longer appears in a bold typeface. If you don't want to forget to respond or take action on that e-mail, you can mark it as "unread" and change the font back to bold.

Any unread e-mail also displays in your *Unread Mail* folder. With just a click on that folder, you can quickly see all unread e-mail items that require action. You can mark an e-mail as unread by:

1. **Selecting** the e-mail you want to mark as unread by clicking on it once.
2. **Selecting** the **Unread/Read** button.

Or

1. **Right-Clicking** on the e-mail you want to mark as unread.
2. Selecting **Mark as Unread.**

Flagging E-Mail for Follow Up for Yourself and Others before *the E-Mail Is Sent*

Setting the follow-up flag for you and/or the recipient *before* you send an e-mail will ensure that you don't forget to follow up on a time-sensitive e-mail or one that requires a response. Instead of going to your **Sent** file to look for the e-mail, you will instead see the e-mail in your **Reminder** box.

While we know that everyone is busy and that it takes time to follow up, doing so is an important part of business—and using these steps will save you time in the future. People with whom you correspond may not be accustomed to responding in a timely fashion. If you need a reply from them to close a piece of business or take the next action, you may want to consider setting the follow-up flag for you and/or the recipient. This will remind you to check in, and/or remind them to respond.

Here's How It Works

1. Open a new e-mail message.
2. Click the **Follow Up** button.
3. Select **Custom**. A **Custom dialog box** opens (Figure 18.3).
4. Decide if you will flag for yourself, the recipient, or both. From the **Flag to** drop-down list, select what follow-up action you need to take from the following options: Call, Do Not Forward, Follow Up, For Your Information, Forward, No Response Necessary, Read, Reply, Reply to All, or Review.
5. Set your **Start date** and **Due date**.
6. Click in the **Reminder** box, and set a day and time for your reminder.

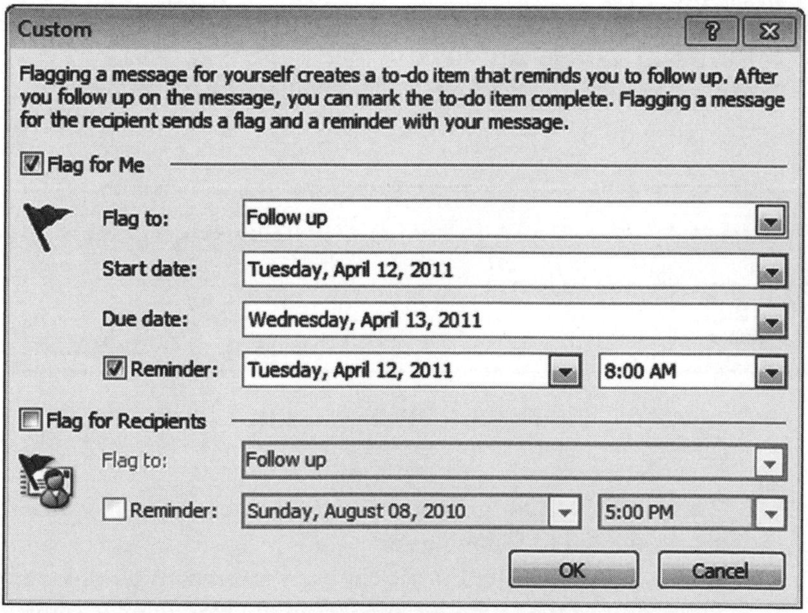

Figure 18.3   Flagging a Message to Yourself

Tip: Set the reminder to appear at the time you get into the office, so you can review all of your reminders first thing.

1. If you are going to set a flag for your recipient, click in the **Flag for Recipients** box, and then set the **Flag to,** along with the reminder date and time.
2. Compose your e-mail and press **Send**.
3. Your **Reminder dialog box** will display all reminders, whether they are for a task, an appointment, a contact, or an e-mail (Figure 18.4). You will notice in the screen capture that each reminder has an icon next to it.

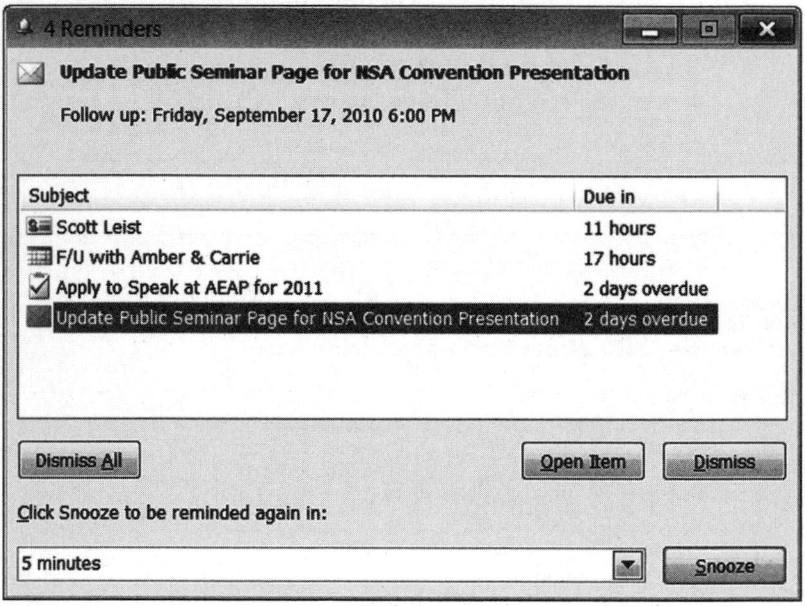

Figure 18.4   Reminder Box

4. This allows you to quickly determine which ones are e-mails that you need to follow up on.
5. If you know that the e-mail has been taken care of, you can either dismiss the reminder, or you can double-click the e-mail to open it and then delete it.

6. If the e-mail still requires follow-up, double-click to open and forward back to the recipient to check in—and don't forget to reset the reminder flags before you press Send!

Tip: If you plan to set a follow-up flag on an e-mail before you send it, I recommend that you take this step first when you open a new e-mail. This will keep you from accidentally pressing Send without setting the reminders. Once they're sent, you can't set them without resending the e-mail.

Tip: Get in the habit of checking your Reminder box daily. If you don't see the Reminder box, go to the **View** menu and select **Reminders Window**.

Maintaining a Follow-Up Flag System

Any system you create is only as good as the commitment you make to maintain it. If you start flagging a bunch of e-mails for follow-up but never set aside the time to *actually follow up*—then there really is no point in setting the flag in the first place.

Organizing E-Mail Using Folders

I wrote about a system for processing e-mail on a regular basis earlier in the chapter. You'll recall that I instructed you to think of your e-mail inbox like your inbox for paper. You wouldn't leave papers in your inbox of hard-copy material that need to be recycled, shredded, forwarded, or filed; you'd put them in the proper location. Your e-mail inbox is no different.

Think of your inbox as a big filing cabinet with several drawers, lots of hanging files, and even more file folders in those hanging files. You can re-create an e-mail system that is similar to the one you've created for your paper-based files. In fact, I recommend doing so. You can then re-create parts of the file structure you use in one location for another area.

Creating Folders in Your Inbox. While this step is fairly simple, it can be somewhat challenging to determine the structure that will work best for you.

Here's How You Create Folders and Subfolders
1. Right-click on the folder called Inbox.
2. From the submenu, click **New Folder**.
3. Enter a folder name.
4. Click **OK**.

The example you see in Figure 18.5 is my inbox filing structure at the highest level.

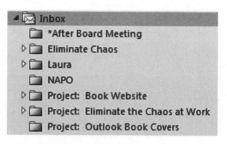

Figure 18.5　　Inbox Filing Structure—Highest Level

Think of the first level of file folders as *filing cabinets* in your Inbox filing system. I typically have a minimum of three folders: one for work, one for personal, and one for volunteer work. I currently have four folders in addition to these: three for current projects and one temporary file. I will explain each file type and idea.

I—like most other people—typically work on a number of projects during the same time frame: I do not want to have to continually open the Eliminate Chaos filing cabinet (or in this case—expand the folder) that contains all e-mails relevant to the projects in order to file something; I just want to file it and move on. This system allows me the flexibility to do so. When the project is complete, I move the entire folder to the Eliminate Chaos folder. Because each of my Project files starts with the word *Project*, I can be assured that they will all be filed next to each other in the Eliminate Chaos drawer.

The other type of file I create is what I call a *temporary* file. As seen in the screen shot in Figure 18.6, the *After Board Meeting folder is a place for me to temporarily place e-mails that require action, but that I can't address while I'm traveling. I simply move e-mails that require action to this file until I've returned to the office. Once I've returned, I pull all of those e-mails back into my Inbox to process them. This

Figure 18.6   Temporary File—*After Board Meeting

allows me to see at a glance only those items in my Inbox that I know I can tackle while I'm traveling.

Temporary files work well for collecting responses to specific requests, tracking orders or items purchased online, or for e-mails to which you may need to return at a later date (for example, e-mails you can't respond to if you are traveling). You can mark your temporary files with an * or other symbols such as @, +, ~, or #; I just happen to prefer the *. Putting an * at the beginning of the folder name displays that folder at the top of your inbox filing structure, since these characters are recognized before letters of the alphabet. If you do create a temporary file in which to place e-mail while you're traveling, I recommend that you move those e-mails back into your inbox when you return to the office. This will keep you from accidentally overlooking them; they will become part of your action items since they are now e-mails in your inbox.

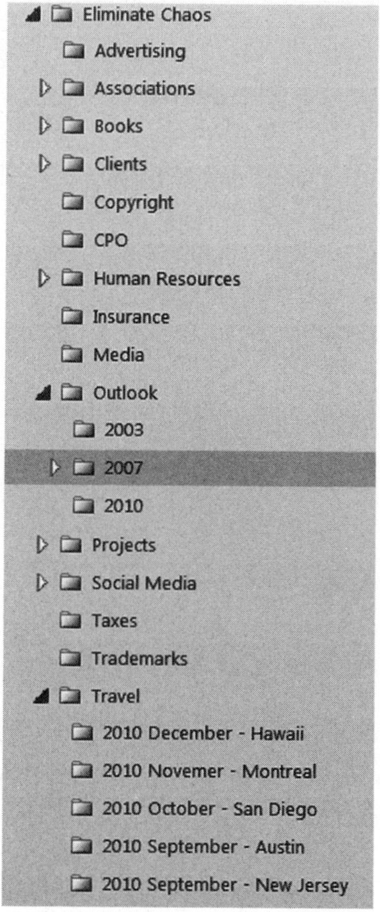

Figure 18.7   Filing Drawers for E-Mail

The e-mail filing cabinet that you use for work can be named whatever makes the most sense for you; for me, **Eliminate Chaos** works best. When you expand the filing cabinet to the next level, you will see the filing *drawers*—or in e-mail terms, the subfolders. Each of these filing drawers may contain additional files and subfiles (Figure 18.7). Think about opening a filing drawer with hanging files inside; you may have one or several folders inside these files. Your e-mail file structure is no different. Folders with an arrow pointing toward them contain subfiles, and some of these folders also contain additional files.

Expanding a few of the folders in the Eliminate Chaos filing cabinet allows you to see their associated subfolders. The downward pointing arrow shows the files that have been expanded, which also contain subfiles. Those subfiles that also have an arrow pointing toward them contain subfolders as well. As you can see, it's important to start at the highest level and think about how your work is structured. Is it more people-, project-, or operations-based, or is it a combination of these activities? Your filing structure will surely look different from the next person's; however, the more *structure* you can give to this, the easier it will be for you to file *and* retrieve information when needed. There are a number of ways to organize your subfolders to

Figure 18.8 Subfolders with Date-Driven Naming Conventions

keep them in order. For example, you may wish to start files in folders with date-driven projects or travel with the year or month (as seen in the **Vacations** folder example in Figure 18.8).

Personal E-Mail File Structure

A personal folder is used to keep personal items separate from work; I call my personal folder **Laura**. I use a structure similar to the one I created for work e-mails, and my personal folder is no different—with the exception of having far fewer files. Again, think of the general categories in your life, and then expand those files with subfolders. I am fairly ruthless with the amount of personal e-mails I keep; I almost always assume that I can obtain the information elsewhere at a later date, should I need it. However, there will always be information that I need to keep, for example, correspondence with tenants of a rental property, copies of my filed tax return with the IRS, hotel and flight arrangements for upcoming vacations, or correspondence about my upcoming destination wedding. I don't need any of this information to live in my inbox; therefore, these files provide a place to keep the information organized and easy to retrieve. Your personal filing structure may look very different, depending on family members, activities, or personal projects. Whether you keep these e-mails on your personal computer or at work, you need a place to store this information where it's separate but easily retrievable. If it's worth keeping, it's worth spending the time to create an effortlessly navigated, simple-to-use structure.

Be sure you understand your company's policy on this before you use your work e-mail account to store personal e-mail. Always remember that e-mail you delete can still be retrieved. Therefore, if it is truly *personal,* think twice before you do personal business at work.

Project E-Mail File Structure

As seen in the original filing structure, there are three project files (Figure 18.9). Keep these project files at the highest level so that they are easily accessible for quickly filing e-mails that you must keep pertaining to the project.

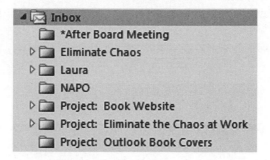

Figure 18.9   Project Files

As with other files, project files each contain subfiles (Figure 18.10). If you think of your project e-mails in terms of paper that you'd file in a binder with several divided sections, it will be easy for you to subdivide your project e-mail folders into these sections. Resist the urge to store all project-related e-mails in the same project file, unless it is an extremely small project.

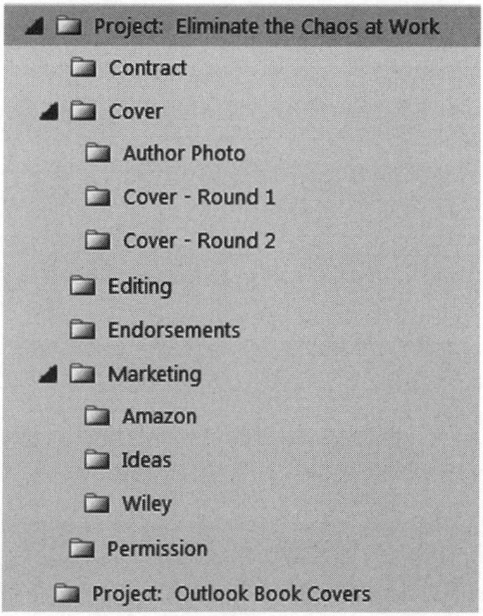

Figure 18.10   Subfiles in a Project File

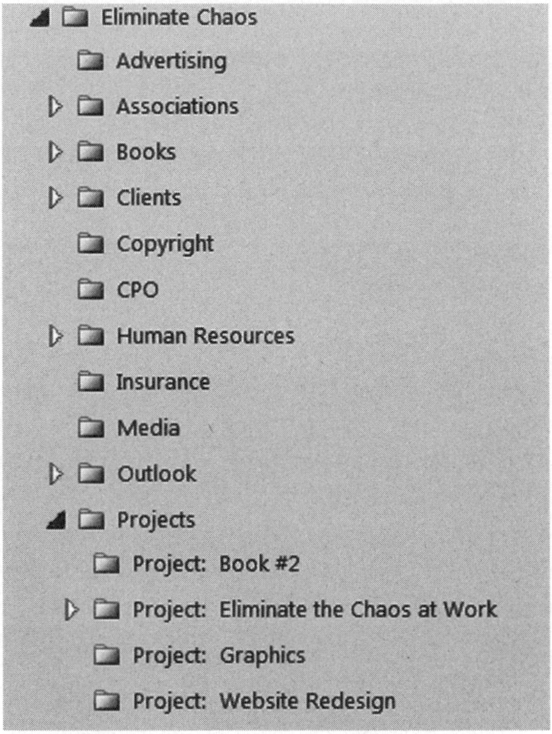

Figure 18.11   Filing Completed Projects

There are two things you should do once you've completed a project. First, take a quick look through the e-mail folder to see if you can eliminate any e-mails. Then, move the Project file to your work filing cabinet, as seen in Figure 18.11. The Project file becomes the location where completed projects live, in case you need to refer to them in the future.

The ways in which you can organize e-mail you must keep are endless; there is no right or wrong way to set up your Inbox filing structure. The key is simply to create a structure that you will use consistently.

Creating and Using E-Mail Templates

Do you ever get tired of typing the same message over and over again, and wish there was a simpler and faster way to get your message out without reinventing the wheel each time? Well, guess what—there is! You can create an e-mail User Template that you can use again and again and again. My colleagues and I utilize these templates on a daily basis in our office. They ensure that we sent consistent communication to prospects and clients, along with other various requests received on a regular basis. I know that some people recommend using the Drafts folder or creating a Signature for e-mail messages that have the same content that are sent on a regular basis—but why do this when the user templates were designed for this specific purpose?

You Can Create a User Template by Taking the Following Steps

1. Open a new e-mail and compose your message.
2. If the e-mail you compose typically includes attachments that *do not* need to be modified or customized in each instance, insert them as an attachment to your template. If you always include the same attachment, you won't need to navigate to your hard drive or server to include the attachment.
3. Select **File Save As**.
4. In the **Save As** dialog box, at the bottom you will see the **Save as type:** with a drop-down list box as shown in Figure 18.12.

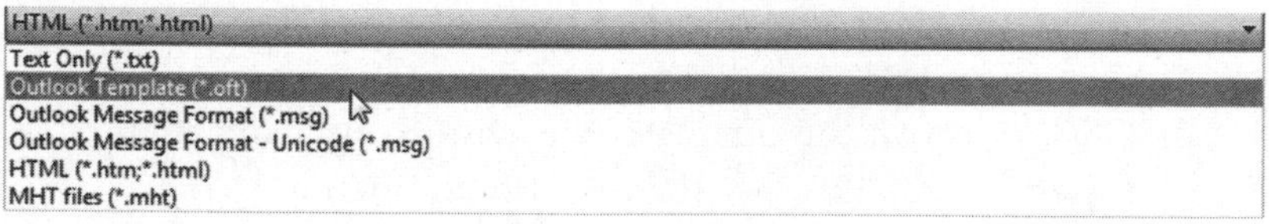

HTML (*.htm;*.html)
Text Only (*.txt)
Outlook Template (*.oft)
Outlook Message Format (*.msg)
Outlook Message Format - Unicode (*.msg)
HTML (*.htm;*.html)
MHT files (*.mht)

Figure 18.12   Types of Formats in Which E-Mails Can Be Saved

5. Select **Outlook Template** from the list.
6. Enter as descriptive a name as possible for your template in the **File name** text box. One good way to name your templates is by using the same name that you would use in the **Subject** line.
7. Click **Save**.
8. Close the e-mail you just saved as an Outlook Template.

9. When prompted to save changes, click **No**. Since you've already saved it as a template, there is no need to save again.

Using Your User Templates

Once you've created your user templates, you are ready to use them.

1. Click on the **New Items** button (Figure 18.13).

New Items ▾

Figure 18.13   The New Items Button

2. From the menu, select **More Items**, and then from the submenu select **Choose Form** (Figure 18.14).
3. A **Choose Form** dialog box (Figure 18.15) opens.
4. From the **Look In:** drop-down list, select **User Templates in File System**.
5. A list of all of the templates you've created will be listed (Figure 18.16).
6. Click once on the template you wish to use, and then click **Open**; or double-click the template to open it.
7. Your e-mail template is now shown on your screen.
8. If you need to modify the e-mail before sending, do so now by making any modifications to the e-mail text or attaching any files.

    Note: If you do make modifications, know that you are not changing the *template*—only the particular e-mail that you are sending. To modify the template, you need to follow the directions in the **Creating a User Template** section.
9. If you don't need to make any modifications, enter a name in the **To** field and press **Send**.

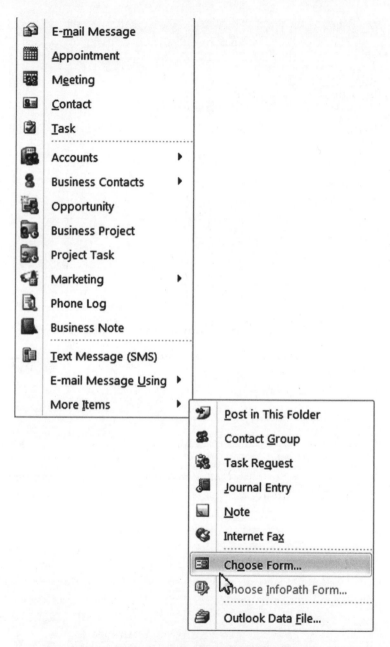

Figure 18.14 Selecting Choose Form

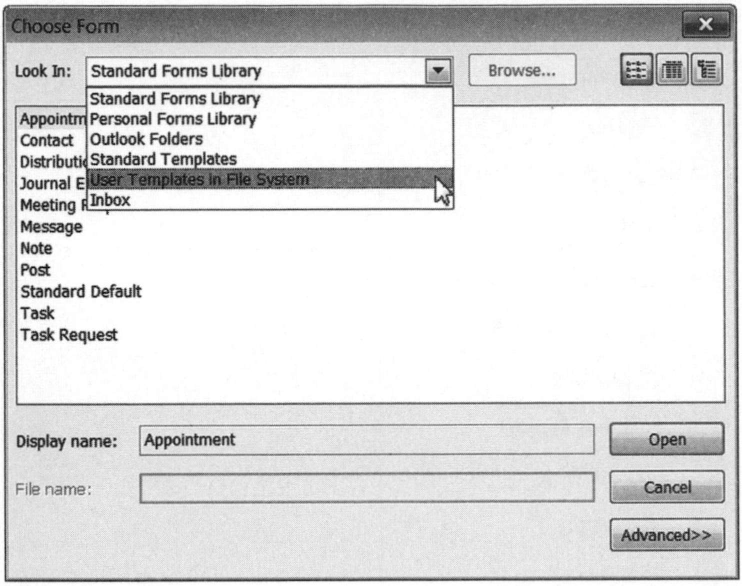

Figure 18.15   The Choose Form Dialog Box

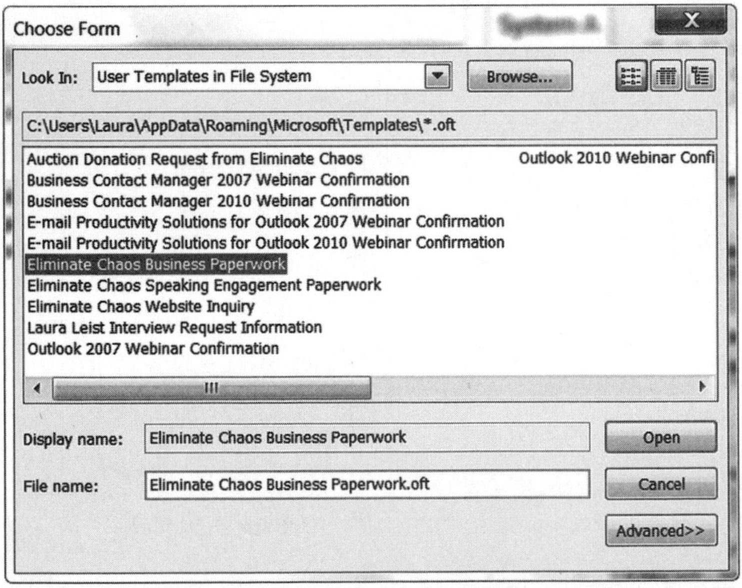

Figure 18.16   List of Templates

User Templates versus a Draft E-Mail

You've probably encountered the Drafts folder (Figure 18.17) in your Mailbox before. This is where e-mails are temporarily stored when you are working on them. Clicking the Save button when you're composing an e-mail will also save the e-mail in the Drafts folder.

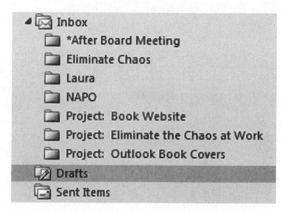

Figure 18.17   The Drafts Folder

While you can certainly store e-mail that you wish to use again and again in the Drafts folder, you will need to copy and paste the text to a new e-mail each time in order for a copy of the e-mail to remain in the Drafts folder. E-mails stored in the Drafts folder for future use will not retain a copy in the Drafts folder if you send it to someone. This is why I recommend that you create User Templates for e-mails you send repeatedly. This keeps you from running the risk of deleting a user template from your directory unless you have deliberately navigated to it and deleted it.

E-Mail Rules

Another way to keep e-mails to a minimum in your Inbox is to use **Rules**. Rules can automatically move e-mail from your inbox to a subfolder based on specific criteria that you select. Rules work well for e-mails that are of an informational nature and that do not require an immediate—or any—response. I could devote an entire chapter to all of the various rules options. However, since I do not have that amount of space, I'm just going to provide you with a basic understanding of how to go about creating a rule. You can then spend more time determining how rules might work best in your particular work environment.

1. Click on the **Rules** button (Figure 18.18).

Figure 18.18   The Rules Button

2. The **Create Rule** dialog box opens where you will begin to create your rules. As you can see from the screen capture in Figure 18.19, I have opted to select e-mails that contain the

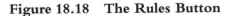

Figure 18.19   The Create Rule Dialog Box

words NAPO Listserve in the subject line and move them to a subfolder in my Inbox.

3. When I click in the check box next to **Move the item to folder:** it displays a **Rules and Alerts** dialog box (Figure 18.20) where I can navigate to the folder to which I want all of these e-mails to automatically be moved once received. After I click on OK, I see a Success dialog box that lets me know that my rule has been created.

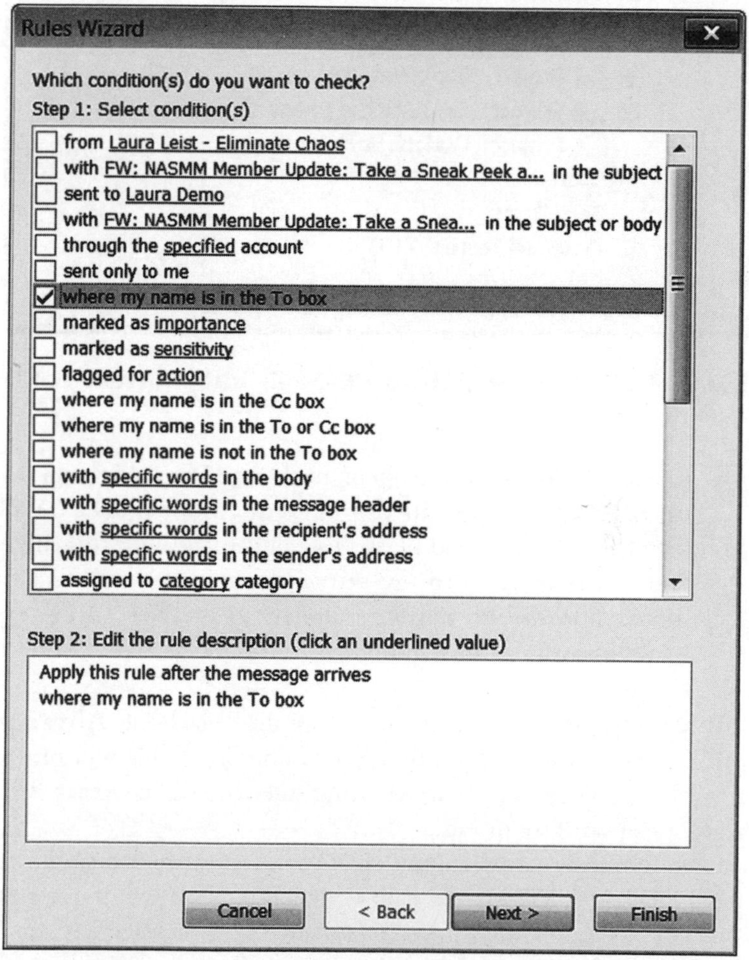

Figure 18.20   Rules and Alerts Dialog Box

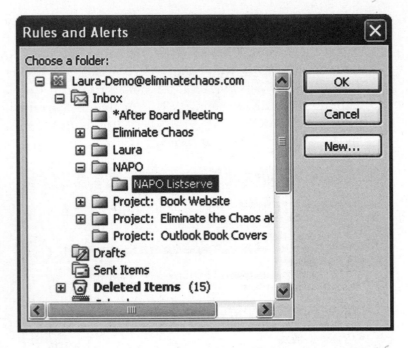

Figure 18.21   Sorting Existing E-Mails into Current Folder

4. I now have the option to check the box to **Run this rule now on message already in the current folder** (Figure 18.21). If I check this box and press **OK,** all e-mails with this subject line will be moved. In the future, any new e-mails with this subject line will be delivered directly to the NAPO Listserve folder instead of to my Inbox.

When creating a new rule, you can also select the **Advanced Options** button on the **Create Rule** dialog box. This will provide you with even more options for creating rules, as you see in the Rules Wizard screen capture in Figure 18.22.

Keep in mind that when you create rules to move e-mail directly to subfolders, you will not see it in your inbox. This will require you to periodically go to the folders to review these messages. It can be easy to overlook; "out of sight, out of mind" applies to e-mail just as much as other areas of our lives.

Figure 18.22   Rules Wizard

Additional Outlook Productivity Resources

Although I have provided information in this chapter about how you can be more productive and organized in using Microsoft Outlook, there's always more to learn, and far more information than I could include here. Additional resources, including books, webinars, seminars, and tips, can be found on our website at www.eliminatethechaosatwork.com.

19 | Considerations When Purchasing a Smartphone

Technique #20: Understand the Questions You Should Ask, and Answer These Questions before You Purchase Your Next Mobile Device

Smartphones or PDAs (personal digital assistants) were designed to enhance, not control, our professional and personal lives. Yet nowadays, these devices not only run our lives, some have also been known to cause accidents, some of which end lives.

I remember the day when I got my first cell phone. It was about two years after I graduated from college, and there was no such thing as a PDA at the time. (If there was, I would've had one, of course; after all, I did graduate with a degree in management information systems.) Today, 1 rarely leave my office or home without this all-important device. While I try extremely hard to not let it control my life, there are days when I'm not too upset if I accidentally forget to turn it back on or if I don't have it with me. Though my Smartphone certainly makes me more productive when I'm not in the office, I don't feel the need to constantly check e-mail, talk on the phone, or text. I personally do not want to be that connected all of the time, and I'm fairly sure that my clients wouldn't be too pleased if I was using it while I was supposed to be working with them. I simply don't need to be online 100 percent of the time in my line of work. However, your situation—and need for electronic communication—will most likely differ from mine and everyone else's. Only *you* can determine how connected you need to be at all times.

Just recently—a few days before I wrote this chapter, in fact—one of my clients said to me: "Can you tell me how I can stop using my BlackBerry in the car?" I'm pretty sure it was partially a joke; after all, in Washington State (where we live), you are not allowed to text, check e-mail, or talk on the phone without a headset. It came as no surprise to me that his BlackBerry controls his life—not just during the day, but on the evenings and weekends as well. While I never got to answer his question because he had moved on to something else, I'm guessing he may not have liked my response. What we did ultimately discuss was that he was—in his own words—"partially to blame" for making himself so accessible during all hours of the day and weekend—especially when his particular line of work did not require this to be the case.

I'm not going to spend a lot of time on the subject of Smart-phones, because everyone's situation and chosen tool is different. However, there are a few points I believe are worth noting—topics that we continually see as challenges in our practice and the clients with whom we consult.

Before I provide you with a list of questions to consider, understand that there are five operating systems for the majority of the mobile devices that are available today: iPhone, Android, BlackBerry, Windows Mobile, and Palm. Your mobile phone's operating system will dictate the types of applications you can use with the smart phone, as well as how you can synchronize data to your device.

Important Questions to Ask Yourself before Purchasing a Mobile Device

1. What nonnegotiable functions do you need your device to perform? If it can't fill one of the primary purposes for purchasing it, you need to continue your search.
2. Do you know how you want to use the device and what you want out of it?
3. What available mobile applications will benefit you the most?
4. Do you know how other systems in your office will integrate with the device you're considering?
5. Has your company standardized on a specific carrier or device? If so, your options will be limited.
6. Is there an Exchange server or Blackberry Enterprise Server with which your Smartphone will sync?
7. How much data do you need to sync from your device each month?
8. What is your annual mobile budget versus your expected ROI in time savings and money savings?

Common Challenges

1. In the past, wireless carriers didn't require you to have lengthy contracts. However, it's now fairly common to have to sign

a two-year plan each time you get a new phone or face a penalty to end the contract early.

2. This kind of contract causes many individuals and companies to feel a level of vendor "lock-in" that prevents them from getting an iPhone or other type of Smartphone until the contract is up.

3. Don't assume that everyone can send or receive texts at a specific phone number. We once had a client become upset because we did not answer a text that was sent to our main office landline. Since our VoIP phone system does not accept texts, we never saw it and therefore could not respond.

4. Unless you are locked in by your company on a specific carrier, don't be afraid to explore the other options out there and jump ship. Determine what the termination fees are; it's certainly preferable to get out of the contract and pay the fee if it means increasing your productivity.

You will be in a much better position the next time you purchase a new Smartphone or renew your contract if you can answer the preceding questions before your purchase. Keep in mind that the salesperson at the store does not understand your business needs if you can't state what they are. Don't buy something because it's the latest and greatest and everyone has one; make your purchase deliberately, and I guarantee that you will fully appreciate the results.

20 | Tools and Resources

Technique #21: Connect to Your Files and Applications Securely from Anywhere via the Internet

Technique #22: Organize and Share Notes, Thoughts, Photos, and Ideas in a Way You Can Find Them

Technique #23: Find Out If a CRM Is Right for You, and Have All the Answers When It Is Time to Implement One

There are far more tools and resources than I can possibly mention in this chapter—or even in this book. My intent is to provide you with a high-level overview of several tools in a variety of categories that you may want to look into further and use at work. Please know that I was not compensated by the companies listed in this chapter; rather, these are tools we recommend to our clients and implement ourselves.

File Sharing

File sharing is a daily challenge in the workplace. The invention of the thumb drive has made it easier than ever to share or take files with you. However, you are bound to run into version control issues at some point or provide your IT department with a headache because of the lack of security this method of file sharing involves. The file-sharing tool you use will have a lot to do with the size of your company and the systems you employ. For solopreneurs and small businesses that do not have a file server or use SharePoint®, I recommend the following:

Drop Box

Drop Box allows you to sync files between your Mac or PC computers and back up files online. A copy is stored here that you can access from any computer, web browser, or mobile device, and a free application for iPhone, iPad, and Android users allows on-the-go access.

Here's an often-encountered problem that Drop Box can help you solve. Let's say you want to e-mail a proposal or other large file but are concerned about whether the recipient will receive your file because of its size and/or any attachment limitations at the receiving company. All you need to do is put your file in your Drop Box public folder, right-click the file to Select–Drop Box–Copy Public Link, paste the link from the file in the public folder into the e-mail message, and e-mail the link to the person you want to receive the file. The recipient clicks on the link in the e-mail and downloads the secure file. If you don't want the recipient to see a lengthy URL in the e-mail you send, highlight the hyperlink in the e-mail and change its text to something that more closely resembles the file name. You have now delivered a file safely, securely, and professionally.

Sugar Sync

This program lets you sync, back up, and access your files anywhere, instantly and securely from a Mac, PC, or mobile device. Sharing a file or directory with Sugar Sync works a bit differently than with Drop Box. When you want to share something, you right-click, share, and then enter the e-mail addresses of the people you want to see the document. Sugar Sync then sends your link. Some users disagree with this delivery method, since Sugar Sync will include marketing material in the e-mail message that contains the link to the file. There is also the privacy issue of providing third-party information to have a file delivered. I am unsure of the timeline, but rumor has it that Sugar Sync might be changing this in the future.

The next two recommendations for file sharing are SharePoint and a file server or file share. Though these tools are typically deployed in larger organizations, there is no reason that a smaller business couldn't use them as well. My company, for example, is a fairly small organization—currently 10 employees—and we have our own file server in the office to use locally, as well as SharePoint to use in the field with clients or when traveling. There are many Internet-based providers that sell hosted SharePoint as a service, typically along with hosted exchange.

File Server

File servers allow you to share files between computers. The advantage they provide is that all company files are stored in a single location that everyone can access and that is backed up on a regular basis. Security can be applied to protect sensitive files; for example, you would not want the Marketing Department to be able to access the Human Resources employee files. During the past few years, file server functions have moved to appliance hardware called network attached storage (NAS). This appliance provides redundancy and security but is more cost efficient than a full PC-based file server. NAS appliances are a less expensive way for both small and large businesses to share files of any size.

SharePoint

Microsoft SharePoint is similar to a file server but has the added benefit of allowing users to access the server from virtually anywhere they have Internet access. SharePoint has additional collaboration ability and can be customized into a full company portal that can not only share files but also contains forms and automated business process logic, providing for automated approval process and notifications. You do not need to worry about costly programming and customizations if you simply want to share files via the web; SharePoint will serve that function reliably.

How to Map a Drive to a SharePoint Site

Instead of logging into the SharePoint website each time you want to access a file, you can create a map to the server that will provide access to the files via the file explorer on a PC.

1. Login to your SharePoint Server via Internet Explorer®.
2. Highlight the URL–right click and select **Copy**. Leave the URL open for now.
3. Click **Start** and select **Computer**.
4. On the bar above, select **Map Network Drive**.

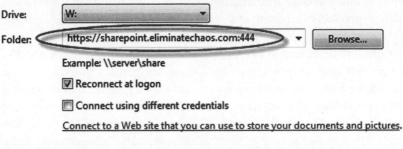

Figure 20.1   Mapping a Network Folder

5. Select an unused drive letter (Figure 20.1).
6. Paste the URL from step 2 into the folder box. Remove everything after and including the slash, for example, https://sharepoint.eliminatechaos.com:444/default.aspx should be changed to have only https://sharepoint.eliminatechaos.com:444 pasted into the folder path (see Figure 20.1).
7. Select **Finish.**
8. Enter your user login and password.
9. You can now access your SharePoint files by clicking on the drive letter you mapped in step 5.

Remote Desktop Services

Remote desktop services allow you to access your computer or information remotely anywhere, anytime. Some of the reasons you may find one of these services useful or necessary are:

- You want to access your Windows PC from your iPad.
- You need to access a local file share remotely from home or another office.
- You need to print something stored in another location on a local printer.

- You have a licensing issue; in other words, the application you are accessing is licensed on only one computer, and you need access to it from another.
- You travel and don't desire to lug your laptop with you since you can access e-mail on your mobile device, but you do need to access a document while you're away.
- You need to work on files that are too large to transfer over the Internet.
- You need to collaborate on a project with someone in a different location.

LogMeIn®

LogMeIn provides remote access to your PC or Mac at any time and from anywhere. It also gives you access to files from your iPhone, iPad, or Smartphone. There are both free and paid versions of LogMeIn tools, and you will not need to modify your firewall to use them. Individual users and small businesses will most likely be able to use the free version. Our clients love the fact that we are able to use this tool to log into their computers and work with them remotely. Not a day goes by in our office when LogMeIn doesn't get used.

GoToMyPC®

Similar to LogMeIn, use this tool from any web browser in real time to access your Mac or PC. You will not need to modify your firewall to use this tool. There is a free 30-day trial for individuals and businesses, and then paid versions of both.

Microsoft Remote Desktop

The Microsoft remote desktop client is on every PC. You will need to open UDP port 3389 on your firewall for this tool to work from outside your network. The disadvantage of accessing the computer by using this approach is that you will not be able to retain the desktop state when you log in. The remote client will create a separate desktop session and log out the existing session, and the user of the current console session is then logged off. Network administrators regularly use this tool; however, given its complexity, it might not be for you. If you want to explore this option further, Google the phrase "Frequently Asked Questions about Remote Desktop."

Note Taking and Archiving Applications and Services

Evernote™

Evernote allows you to capture just about any type of data and quickly locate information. This service works with Macs and PCs, as well as just about any mobile device, including iPhone, iPad, iPod touch, Android, Blackberry, Palm, and Windows Mobile. This service lets you capture text, a webpage or a clip from a webpage, audio files, pdfs, photos, and more. The data that you save sync to your computer, mobile device, and the web, so you can access it wherever you are. You can even retrieve your information when you are off-line. There is a free version, as well as a premium version. For less than $50 per year, you can upgrade to premium and increase your monthly upload size, sync additional file types—such as Microsoft Office docs and video files—and collaborate with others by giving them permission to edit your notes. Hardware, applications, and notebooks have been developed that work with Evernote Trunk. One such application is Nozbe, a to-do list and task manager software that was inspired by David Allen's Getting Things Done (GTD) methodology.

OneNote®

Microsoft OneNote 2010 provides the ability to store, organize, and share your information all in one place. To help you visualize the capabilities of OneNote, think of it as a giant spiral notebook divided into sections, each having a number of pages. These pages let you store text, documents, website links, audio and video files, photos, and screen clippings. You can create multiple OneNote notebooks or just keep one, depending on the content you desire to store. For example, you could have a notebook for work, one for personal, and one for the MBA you're working on. I use three: one called **Eliminate Chaos** for everything work related, one called **Laura** for my personal use, and one for **the National Association of Professional Organizers (NAPO)**, which is the association of which I am the president. My Eliminate Chaos notebook is divided into four sections: Books, Conferences, Projects, and Website Ideas. The Conferences section of the notebook has a page for each association conference I attend, with a subpage for each year I've attended. This is the place where I keep all of my notes, quotes, handouts, conference brochures, and more for reference in the future.

NAPO
2011 - San Diego, CA
2010 - Columbus, OH
2009 - Orlando, FL
2008 - Reno, NV
NSA
2011 - Anaheim, CA
2010 - Orlando, FL
2008 - NYC, NY
NASMM
2011 - St. Pete, FL
2010 - Las Vegas, NV
NSGCD
2010 - Austin, TX

Figure 20.2   Conferences File Structure

The screen capture in Figure 20.2 shows the file structure for my Conferences section. People like me who attend conferences often come back to the office with lots of information—but no idea what to *do* with it. Before OneNote, I kept one small journal book for all conferences I attended, and I created a section for each conference attended. This allowed me to keep all of my information in one place and not have multiple notebooks. But now the process is simplified even more because I have a place to store the notes I take as well as the handouts in one place, instead of looking in two places. Even if you don't attend conferences for your job, I'm sure you can think of many ways to divide your notebooks.

You can store your notebooks on your computer or share them with others on your network or the Internet. Sharing your notebooks lets you simultaneously edit and take notes with others in different locations and see recent changes and who made them when you open a shared notebook. If you have a Windows Mobile phone and SharePoint 2010 or Windows Live, you will be able to access, store, view, and edit information via your phone.

Customer Relationship Management

No business, no matter the size, should be without a customer relationship management tool, or CRM, as it's typically called. A CRM is designed to track e-mail history, phone conversations, follow-up, appointments, client- and project-related tasks, opportunities, and leads, as well as provide the ability to use the data for marketing campaigns, look at the sales pipeline and sales projections, and generate a wide variety of reports based on data contained in your CRM. Before you spend time or money on purchasing and implementing one of these systems—or time and money switching to a new one—you need to be able to answer the following important questions:

1. **What is your exit strategy?** In other words, when you want to convert from one system to another, are you able to export all of your information? We've had clients decide that they want to move from one CRM to another, only to discover they could not export their data from a cloud-based CRM.

2. **What will be your long-term ROI for the CRM you select?** Don't just consider the short-term costs. While cloud-based solutions will look attractive because of a low monthly fee and free upgrades, you need to consider how long you

will use this tool and how many users you'll be paying for per month. The cost will add up quickly—and while the convenience of accessing this information from any computer could prove to be money well spent, you may be able to spend that money on a solution that would allow access to a piece of software installed on a PC with a fixed cost, for example, using a remote desktop tool or a virtual private network (VPN) to connect to the software.

3. **How do you want to use the information that will be stored in the CRM?** If you don't know what the outputs are, it's going to be hard to figure out what the inputs should be and how you will customize the tool to work for your organization.

4. **Do you have buy-in?** What are your plans for ensuring that employees who need to use this tool receive the necessary training based on expectations for its defined objectives? Without buy-in, you run the risk that employees won't use the system because the solution ultimately did not meet the needs required for everyone to perform their job functions. It is vital to meet with the end users and understand both the current and desired business process, as well as what data need to be tracked.

There are CRM software applications, such as Act!, Business Contact Manager for Outlook, and Goldmine, in addition to web-based tools like Saleforce.com, Sugar CRM, and Microsoft Dynamics®. This is by no means a comprehensive list; I am referencing just a few of the more widely used solutions. Web-based or cloud solutions are gaining popularity with small businesses because of their ease of use, technical support, and accessibility from any location. However, it is still imperative that small businesses do their due diligence when selecting a CRM or moving to a new one. As mentioned previously, there is much more to consider than just accessibility.

When I founded Eliminate Chaos, I used Act! as our CRM but made the switch to Microsoft's Outlook Business Contact Manager (BCM), which is designed for small businesses of about 50 users. While we consult on a variety of CRM tools for businesses of all sizes, the one that now best fits our needs is BCM.

I do not have room to write about each CRM listed in this chapter. Since people's needs vary greatly, I recommend that you consider the questions in this section and then complete your research and a cost analysis before you make a purchase and begin implementation and training.

Additional Resources

For additional information on some of these tools, please visit our website at www.eliminatethechaosatwork.com. Here you will also find additional books, webinars, and seminars on Microsoft Outlook, Microsoft Business Contact Manager, and a variety of other tools.

21 | Preparing for a Data Disaster

Technique #24: Implement a Disaster Recovery Plan for Your Electronic Data

The most preventable type of business disaster is the loss of data. According to *Home Office Computing Magazine,* **31 percent** of PC users have lost all of their files due to events beyond their control. Having a backup system does you no good if you don't *use it.* Merely having a plan in place won't solve your problem when a computer crashes or a laptop is stolen. I know you *know* you should back up your electronic information—but if you still haven't gotten around to it, read on. Even if you think the information on your computers is supported by some kind of alternate system, I encourage you to read this chapter. You may discover something you did not consider in the past.

I realize this subject makes a lot of eyes glaze over, but I'm going to do my best to make this as easy as possible to understand. This will allow you to see what some of the issues are and how you can go about resolving them.

It doesn't matter if you work for a large corporation or a small business or are a solopreneur; everyone needs to back up their important files. In fact, your home computer should also be backed up where you store your precious family photos and other information that you may never be able to re-create.

What You Need to Know If You Work at a Large Corporation

Chances are that there's an on-site corporate IT department charged with backing up critical systems and data stored on servers. However, you should be aware that in most companies, IT does not back up your C drive or your My Documents folder. Therefore, if you're saving your documents to one of these places, you're in for a big surprise if anything happens to your computer. I've recently worked with several corporations to help streamline and organize electronic

197

information on their servers, and I found a common theme: Employees never stored any of their files on the server. They merely saved them to their My Documents folder and assumed (incorrectly) that IT had everything backed up. This takes place in companies all too frequently. Employees need to be aware of exactly what material their IT departments back up. One of the best ways to ensure that everyone follows the same guidelines is to implement a company policy that states where documents are to be stored. No one has time or money to re-create lost documents.

If you work in the field and are not always connected to the servers through a VPN (virtual private network) or are often logged in remotely, there are additional steps I encourage you to implement. There are remote backup solutions available for you to purchase for less than $50 a year. (I discuss these in detail a bit later in the chapter.) Even if your employer is not willing to foot the bill, it will cost you the equivalent of only about one latte per month. According to the Federal Trade Commission, more than 10,000 laptops are reported lost every week at 36 of the largest U.S. airports. Your time is worth much more than the $50 you will spend to avoid having to re-create lost information. Check with your IT department if you think a remote backup solution would be ideal for you.

What You Need to Know If You Are a Small Business Owner

As a small business owner, your work computer and personal computer may be one and the same. The two most important files you need to protect are your company accounting file, such as QuickBooks (.qbw), and your e-mail file, such as an Outlook.pst file. Regardless of whether you use these two particular programs, you must back up these two systems—or risk putting yourself out of business if there is a fire or disaster in which your computer is destroyed, crashed, stolen, or simply stops working. Without your accounting file, you will have no idea of what has been invoiced and is owed. Think about how the conversation with the IRS may go when you tell them that you'd love to file your tax return, but you have no data with which to file. I don't think they'll be satisfied with a guesstimate. The third and fourth most important files to back up—if you share a computer for your business and personal use—are your photos and digital music files.

Most small businesses *do not* have a comprehensive backup plan, for two primary reasons: (1) You do not have an IT professional who understands your business needs and has recommended an appropriate plan, or (2) you are trying to save money by failing to address this critical business function. You need to stop thinking about the cost to deploy a solution and instead appreciate the return on investment you'll get countless times over in the future. You should conduct backups and store them off-site daily on each computer. Remote employees or sales professionals need a remote backup solution, as outlined in the next section. If you do happen to be using an Exchange server for e-mail and suffer a drive crash when you recover the computer, your mailbox will fully sync back to your Outlook client. And be sure your server is backed up as well.

Remote Backup Solutions

There are many remote backup solutions available, such as Mozy, Carbonite, and Keepit. Mozy happens to be our organization's favorite (and no, I'm not being compensated to say this). It's a file-level backup system that will restore the files to your computer but not the computer software. If you do not have your operating system software in a safe place, you may need to purchase it again. Though computer companies such as Dell and HP typically install a recovery partition in a separate area of the main hard drive, the reality is that computers often take the recovery partition with them when they go south. The annual cost for Mozy will run you about $50—and always remember that the actual cost of any backup solution will always be less than the cost of potentially lost data and time.

Backup Solutions for Those Who Value Data More Than Money

Taking a backup system one step further to a point-in-time recovery solution will cost you a bit more initially; however, it will end up saving you more time and money than your original investment. A point-in-time recovery system takes a snapshot of your entire computer at a specific time each day, rather than just making a backup of your files. This allows all of your computer files *and* programs to be restored without having to reload software. This kind of tool is especially handy when you need to restore your computer to a new machine or—heaven forbid—can't locate your software. If you ever needed to restore both your files and your programs, you are looking at approximately two hours of work—versus an entire week. Premium Windows 7 and Vista versions have a built-in backup and restore center that provides you with the ability to create a system image, which is an exact image of a drive. You can restore the entire drive (but not individual files) from this. Our office staff makes biannual system images that are stored off-site and uses individual file backups in between. This way, we can recover the entire PC, and then update the changed files if there are any problems.

At Home

There are undoubtedly several files on your home computer that would be difficult if not impossible to replace. Some of the most important files that come to mind are:

- **Personal financial information** stored in a piece of software; though you may be able to re-create some of this information, it's likely to be an extremely time-consuming process.
- **Digital pictures**—how would you ever be able to re-create these memories?
- Your **music library**—you've spent a lot of money to either download the music or have stored your music to your computer and eliminated the CDs.
- **Genealogy information**—like the financial information, you may be able to re-create some, but at a cost of your time.

Sometimes even people who have experts in their family do not take advice. A few months before I wrote this chapter, a relative of mine—who shall remain nameless—had all of her pictures stored on her laptop, and guess what? No backup. In this instance, it wasn't the hard drive that crashed; it was the controller board that fried, and it took the hard drive right along with it, which, in turn, fried all of the laptop's circuitry. After several unsuccessful attempts by an IT professional at her husband's office, the laptop arrived in our office. Our business systems consultant spent more than a day working on it until he was able to restore all of her data—including her pictures—because the drive itself was intact. Can you say "lucky"? Notice to the risk taker: Results may vary, in many cases the moving parts of the drive crash making recovery difficult and expensive. Compressed or encrypted data on a drive are extremely difficult or impossible to recover.

If you have a personal computer at home, don't overlook the need to find a backup solution for yourself and your family. A remote solution will work, as will a USB external hard drive; however, the remote solution will provide more peace of mind than an external hard drive, because the latter with the backup data is sitting next to the same PC. Therefore, it can be damaged or stolen right along with the PC in cases of fire or theft. The remote solution, on the other hand, allows you to set it and forget about it—since it's in an entirely different location.

Do You Know Where Your Software Is Stored?

Could you put your hands on software in your office at any given moment? If not, I recommend that you create a location where software is stored in an organized fashion—because when the time comes, the last thing you want to do is waste precious minutes searching for it. This is a problem I've seen time and again, for everyone from large IT departments to small businesses to homeowners. We have consulted with and provided hands-on organizing services for a wide variety of companies that had no idea where the most current software was stored. You don't need a fancy solution; you just have to make certain that you identify a specific location, and that others who need to know are informed of this location. Something as simple as a binder with CD pockets will work; you can label the front of the pockets with a software name and product key to ensure that you or someone else knows where to return the software *and* has the product key if it's needed to reinstall the software.

If you took the time to save the information, picture, or music in the first place, you probably want the peace of mind to know that you'll always be able to access this information. Not having a backup system is like not having insurance for your home or car. The time will come when you will need it—and you'll certainly be glad you have it.

IV | Organizing the Stuff

22 | The 10-Step Process to Organize Your Work Space or Office

Technique #25: Use the Eliminate Chaos 10-Step Process as Your Guide to Create the Organized Spaces You Desire in Your Office

In the introduction, I defined *stuff* as anything that must live in the office that is not paper. When people begin to face their need to get organized, they often consider the visible stuff that needs organizing. After all, it's easy upon *seeing* certain things to realize that they're disorganized. However, after reading thus far, you understand that getting organized and being more productive at work can go hand-in-hand—and that being more productive at work goes beyond being visibly organized. So far, I discussed many of the nonvisible systems necessary to design, implement, and maintain in order to remain productive each day.

The last section of this book focuses specifically on how to organize this stuff. Whatever organization project you take on—whether it's in your office, the front reception area, the lunchroom, mail room, office supply room, a storage area, workshop, or warehouse—you will be successful if you follow the 10-step process I have developed and will introduce shortly. I previously outlined this process in my 2006 book, *Eliminate Chaos: The 10-Step Process to Organize Your Home & Life* (Sasquatch Books). While my previous publication covers methods to organize your home, it is the process that counts—and that doesn't change. The very same steps can be used in the office environment to organize the office areas we've already discussed—and then some.

The 10-step process I share with you here works equally well in the office or home office environment—provided that you understand the steps and complete them in the order listed. Where this process will come into play and be the most beneficial is when you are organizing the stuff in your office. You can use this process in almost any situation—whether you are organizing the stuff in your home office or a specific area of your work environment. It doesn't matter which area you plan to tackle first; the following 10 steps will work in any of these areas, and more.

So—let's get started.

Step 1: Dedicate Time

How many times have you said to yourself, "I'll get organized . . . *someday*"? I don't know about you, but the calendar I use does not have a "Someday" at all during the week. Working in an organized office or being able to use an organized space at work is a work-style choice you *make*. In other words, you must identify this goal as a priority and make time to complete it. You will never find the time to get organized (as I hear so many people proclaim).

When I say "dedicate time," what I mean is that I want you to plan this activity on your calendar and schedule an appointment with yourself to work on the particular area you selected. Think of this time as an investment in your personal productivity and work-style. Keep in mind that your project may require more than this initial appointment. You need to continue scheduling time periods during which to complete the task; otherwise, it will be too easy to find something else that is more enjoyable to work on. Though this is a simple concept, so many fail to accomplish this goal—simply because they did not dedicate time and make it a priority.

After you plan the time for this project, make it a priority; resist the urge to reschedule this meeting with yourself, should another event arise. Additional obligations will always surface; if you keep putting this off, it will never get done. Just as you plan time for a meeting or to work on a project, this should be viewed as a project as well.

In my experience with clients over the years—and as you've read previously—this process typically takes longer than you estimate, since those "four-hour miracles" are few and far between. If you think your project is going to take two hours, plan for four. If you think it'll be 8 hours, plan for 16, and break it up into several smaller goals that you can accomplish over a period of time. If you find that you often have trouble making decisions, multiply the amount of time you think it will take you to complete a project by three; that will give you a realistic estimate. Organizing is a process that requires you to make many decisions—some of which will be simple and quick to make, while others will be more challenging and time-consuming. It's important to be properly prepared in terms of the time you think your project will take.

Step 2: Gather Supplies

Gathering supplies is often confused with step 8, which is shopping. Think of shopping as the reward you've earned by doing the hard work up front. The supplies to gather initially are:

- A garbage can—better get a large one with extra bags
- A recycle bin
- Boxes for sorting or donations
- Something to write with and some sticky notes
- Wear comfortable clothing that you're not afraid to get dusty or dirty

With your supplies gathered, you are just about ready to begin your project.

Step 3: Establish a Staging Area

Establishing an area where you can spread out what you are organizing will help you see quantities of items to be organized. Without ample space, you will end up shuffling things around and most likely overlook something. You need space to work in and on, so if horizontal surfaces are at a premium, you may need to create some. The last thing you want to do is put too much on the floor and trip over something and break a foot. Trust me when I say this—because I've been there and done that.

Make sure that that space you've chosen has enough room to spread things out. Not only will it keep you from stepping over things; you will also find it much easier to see what you have and are sorting.

Step 4: Sort

Sorting—one of the most important steps in organizing—is the phase that will make you feel like you have finally begun the organizing process. You must be able to see and know what you have in order to organize, which won't happen unless you sort through your belongings. Though the next two steps—"eliminate" and "group like items together"—can be done at one time, it is important that each of the three steps takes place.

Beginning the sorting process can be one of the most overwhelming steps for people, because it is difficult to know where to start. To keep the sorting process as painless as possible, remember the following: There is no right or wrong way to begin. You just need to pick a place and dive on in. Eventually, you are going to touch everything in the area that you are organizing anyway, so it does not matter where you start. If the room you are organizing is bursting at the seams, then it is even more important for you to establish the staging area, so that you can remove items from the room and create additional space in which to work. Don't worry that you're making an even bigger mess as you begin to sort; I do this all the time when I work with clients, and I can guarantee that everything will eventually find a home. Sometimes just starting at the door, picking up the item closest to you, and making a *decision* on that item is the best place to begin.

Ah—*decisions*—that loaded word. Let's take a brief moment to discuss the process of sorting and decision making. You will discover as you begin that organizing is all about decision making. You need to determine what exactly you are going to do with the item. Think of the clutter around you as delayed decisions that will ultimately result in even more clutter.

As you pick up each item, decide whether you are going to keep, donate, sell, recycle, or throw it away. If you opt for the last choice, put it in the garbage immediately before you allow yourself to touch and pick up the next item. If the item is to be donated, place it in the donations box. If you are keeping it, start establishing areas where you can begin to group like items together. The idea here is to make the decision about the item and follow through before moving on to the next item. Sorting this way will allow you to complete follow-through with that item and resist the urge to look at the next item until you've decided. Remember, follow-through is the key here.

Tip: You may want to set up more than one donations box, since you may have several places you're planning to donate to. This will be much more efficient than putting all of your donations in one box and sorting them later on.

Tip: When sorting, you may want to pick one desk drawer, bookshelf, cabinet, or box of stuff at a time to begin with. Be sure to complete the drawer, bookshelf, cabinet, or box before moving on to the next area.

Step 5: Eliminate

Items that no longer serve a purpose, have little to no value, or are damaged are candidates for the recycle bin, trash, or donate piles. Be realistic as you go through this process; you don't need to keep everything. If you do, you will soon run out of space for things—and they will begin to stack up around you.

Here are some decision-making questions to ask yourself as you are going through this process:

Financial and Legal Questions
Does it belong to you?
Am I legally required to keep it?
Is there a tax reason to keep it?
Will this help me make or save money?
Would I buy it again?
Does it take more time and effort to manage than it is worth?
Would you pay to have it packed and moved if you moved your office?
What does it cost you to keep, store, and maintain it?
Can you get a deduction if you donate it?
What could you do with the money if you sell it?

Practical Questions
Is it useful?
Is it a duplicate?

Is this the best place for it?

Will you remember you have it if you keep it?

Will you be able to find it if you remember you have it?

How are you going to store it or use it?

Do you have room for it?

Do you need it or just want it—or neither?

How long do you need to keep it? When can you get rid of it?

Is it broken or unidentifiable?

Is the information still current?

Will you actually use it or refer to it?

When is the last time you used it?

When do you think you will use it again (or for the first time), and what circumstances will have to be in place for you to use it?

Does this add value to your business currently?

Can it easily be duplicated or created if needed again?

Can you borrow or purchase another one if needed?

What's the worst that can happen if you toss it?

Will you really read it?

Are you going to finish the related project? If so, when?

If you are having a hard time making a decision as to whether you can let something go, place it in a box. When the box is full, tape it up so that it is difficult to get into. Put a "Toss or Donate" date on the box for three months into the future. If you have not found yourself needing to tear into the box for something by the time that date arrives, then it is time to let the items in the box go. Resist the urge to open it again, since you may find yourself back at square one, wondering if you might need these things someday. Now, get rid of the box; I guarantee you will not miss the contents. In all of my years of working with clients, I can recall only two instances when clients wished they had kept something—and both were for sentimental reasons. People typically tell me they do not miss anything they have tossed, donated, or sold—and that most of the time, they cannot even remember what it was they eliminated!

Tip: Use the one-in, one-out method. For every new item you bring into the office, eliminate one item. This will keep space from ever becoming an issue.

Tip: Make it a habit to go through your office or work area at least once or twice annually. You will be surprised how much you accumulate during this time period. Keep a donation location in your office set up year around. If you have office supplies or the like that you will not use, find a nonprofit organization or school that needs these supplies and donate the box when it's full.

Step 6: Group Like Items Together

As you are sorting and eliminating, you will, of course, come across items that you need to keep. The items you are keeping should be placed in groups of like items, which will make the next two steps—Examine Your Space and Shopping—easier for you.

Grouping like items together is the same thing as determining categories of items that will live in your office, workspace, or common office area. This step will tell you how much you have in each category, so that you can make the best use of your space. When organizing and finding new homes for things, you want to ensure that you have enough space for the desired items in the particular location you've chosen. This will be a challenge if you don't group items together. Following are some examples of categories you may find in your home office, work office, or common area.

Supply Room
Copy paper and note pads
Sticky notes and sticky flags
Pens, Sharpies, pencils, highlighters
Binders, dividers, and sheet protectors
Toner
Computer labels
Company letterhead and envelopes
Paper clips, binder clips, staples, rubber bands, tape
Staplers, hole punches, scissors
Office organizing products such as inboxes, stacking desk trays,
    desk organizers, book ends, magazine files
Cleaning products
Mailing and shipping supplies

Your Workspace
Project and client files
A reasonable amount of office supplies
Books and other reference materials
Magazines and journals
Personal items
Personal memorabilia, such as pictures, awards, or certificates
Snacks

Lunch Room
Coffee, tea, hot chocolate, and related supplies
Paper goods, such as napkins, paper towels, paper plates
Plastic ware
Dishes and silverware
Cleaning supplies
Small appliances such as coffee pot, microwave, toaster oven, toaster
Company-provided snacks
Serving dishes for company gatherings

Conference Room
White board markers and erasers
Paper
Writing instruments
Stapler, paper clips, binder clips, rubber bands, tape
Sticky notes
Coffee supplies, such as mugs, spoons, sugar, creamer

Mail Room
Shipping supplies, such as envelopes, mailers, boxes, tape, labels, bubble wrap, packing peanuts
Stamps and dispensers
Scale and postage meter
Utility knives and letter openers
Literature and mail sorters
Paper and company stationery
Small amount of office supplies, such as paper clips, binder clips, staples, writing instruments

Step 7: Examine Your Space

As you begin to map out the space you have available, you need to decide what purpose each space and room will serve. Ask yourself if the existing space or room works for what you are organizing, since it occasionally becomes necessary to use space differently. Think outside the box for a moment; try to forget how you've used this area in the past. Since you're working on a new solution for the future, it's perfectly okay to use the space differently going forward. Consider how often you use certain items in the room or area you're organizing; make sure that those are the most accessible when you are finished with your project.

Once you decide on the general location for the items you've sorted and categorized, it is time to take a good look at what is left. This will help you determine how you will use the remaining space, and what type of products you'll need to purchase to complete your organizing project. Now is the time to start making your list of products that you will need to help organize and store what you are keeping.

Before You Dash Off to the Store or Begin Filling Your Online Shopping Cart:

1. **Measure** the existing space in which you are working, and remember to use those measurements when shopping.
2. If necessary, **draw a diagram** of the room on a piece of paper with the dimensions written down so that you can show it to a salesperson.
3. If you are looking for a specific product, such as drawer organizers, **measure each drawer individually** and **make a brief list** of the contents for each drawer. This will allow you to buy dividers that hold all of your things in the best manner possible.
4. If you are purchasing products to help contain items on a shelf, take the width and depth measurements and check to see if the shelf height is adjustable.

Remember: Before you dash off to the store, you *must* have a plan for the space and a good understanding of how much stuff you need to store and organize. This will save you a lot of valuable time and money by allowing you to purchase what you need the first time—and not have to revisit the store again and again to get items you forgot (because they were not written down) or did not fit (because you did not measure).

Step 8: Shop

Shopping! Did you think you would never make it to this point? Congratulations on resisting the urge to run out to the store and start shopping right away. I know that shopping is the most enjoyable of the 10 steps for many individuals. However, you need to wait until step 8 to begin shopping because you really do not have a good idea of what will be left to be organized until you complete steps 4 to 6 when you embark on an organizing project. Had you shopped at the beginning of this process, you might have acquired products that no longer made sense for what was left to organize or for the space you dedicated to those items. Purchasing organizing supplies at the beginning of a project is like putting a square peg into a round hole; it simply does not work. So save yourself time, money, and frustration, and wait until this phase to hit the stores.

There are thousands of organizing products available today to serve just about any need you have. Make sure you purchase those that will be used and that expressly serve your purposes.

Step 9: Install Product

The second to final step is to install any product that has been purchased. This can be as simple as putting items in appropriate containers and placing them where they will live. It can also be more time-intensive and complicated, should you choose to install new furniture, shelving systems, mail-sorting systems, or a variety of other office products. This is also the point when you will be putting any remaining items that you are keeping into place—with or without organizing products. For most organizing projects, you will probably want to purchase at least a few products to help contain and organize your space.

Step 10: Maintain

Maintenance is one of the most important steps of any organizing project. You've made the work-style choice to operate in an organized and efficient office; for that reason, you need to make it part of your routine to maintain it. Failing to keep up with the newly organized areas or systems and processes that you've implemented will cause you to quickly revert to a less productive environment.

The interval at which you must conduct maintenance varies from one office and process to another. You may need to undertake some procedures on a daily basis; others can be completed weekly, biweekly, or monthly. You will be the judge of the frequency here. This type of maintenance is no different than going on a diet and sustaining your new weight. You have to work at it every day, or the weight will come back. Similarly, should you fail to maintain your new system and organized space, the system will break down over time—and you may eventually wind up right back where you started.

Some Examples of Maintenance

Paper Management Systems: Stay up-to-date on your filing of project- or client-related documents. It's not enough to just create the filing structure and label the folder; you must keep the appropriate papers in them in order to quickly retrieve information when needed. At some point, you'll have to determine what is still worth keeping in hard-copy format—or at all.

Electronic Information Management: Once you've established naming conventions and version control properties for your electronic files, you and/or your coworkers need to maintain these conventions; otherwise, your documents will quickly get out of control. Implementing a CRM is of no value if you and/or your employees are not using it to keep customer information current.

Stuff Management: Haphazardly leaving things in places they do not belong will quickly contribute to clutter in any office or workspace. As much as we'd like to think that there is an office-organizing fairy that floats around, picking things up and putting them in their proper places—they don't exist.

Failure to stay on top of this for a period of time will result in disorder. And it's not enough to just stay on top of it on a regular basis; you should also reexamine your work spaces at least twice a year.

Maintenance can mean a lot of different things depending on the systems you have implemented and the areas you are organizing. Whether maintaining your new system takes five minutes per day or five hours per week, only *you* will be able to determine how much time you will need. This upkeep must be part of your routine if you want to continue to work more productively.

About the Author

Laura Leist, CPO, is a productivity consultant, speaker, and author. In 2000, Laura founded Eliminate Chaos®, an organizing and productivity services firm specializing in electronic information systems management, paper management, and office organization. Laura has a degree in Management Information Systems from Washington State University and more than two decades of experience as a business process and productivity consultant. She works with Fortune 500 companies as well as small businesses to increase productivity and streamline processes. In addition, Laura is an authentic, down-to-earth, and entertaining speaker who provides realistic advice through her seminars and training—each packed full of substance and content. Everyone leaves her presentations inspired to act and armed with the tools and easy-to-implement processes to succeed.

Laura is the author of five books on Microsoft Outlook that she uses as the basis for her Outlook consulting, customization, and training: *Organizing Your Workday Using Microsoft Outlook 2007, E-Mail Productivity Solutions for Microsoft Outlook 2007, Business Solutions Using Outlook 2007 with Business Contact Manager, Organizing & Customizing with Microsoft Outlook 2003,* and *Organizing & Customizing with Microsoft Outlook 2002.* She is currently working on a series for Microsoft Outlook 2010. In addition to these books, Laura is the author of *Eliminate Chaos: The 10-Step Process to Organize Your Home & Life* (Sasquatch Books, 2006).

The media often turn to Laura for her practical and results-oriented advice. Some of the publications she has been quoted in are the *New York Times,* the *Wall Street Journal, Entrepreneur, Woman's*

Entrepreneur, Inc., Real Simple, Family Circle, Woman's Day, Health, and *Better Homes & Gardens.*

Laura is the 2009–2011 president of the National Association of Professional Organizers (NAPO), to which she contributed seven years of service as a board member. She is also the 2009 recipient of the NAPO Shining Star award for her vision and leadership of NAPO's website redesign. Laura is also a past recipient of the *40 Under 40 Award* in 2001, bestowed annually upon 40 entrepreneurs under the age of 40. A member of the National Speaker's Association (NSA), Laura is often asked to speak at their national conventions and conferences for her content-rich productivity expertise.

Laura lives just north of Seattle with her fiancé, their dogs, and a cat.

For more information on hiring Laura or one of the Eliminate Chaos Specialists to consult with your company or speak at your conference or meeting, please connect with us through one of the following methods:

Phone: 425.670.2551
Toll Free: 877.342.8592
Website: www.eliminatethechaosatwork.com
E-Mail: request.information@eliminatechaos.com
Twitter: www.twitter.com/lauraleist
LinkedIn: www.linkedin.com/in/lauraleist
FaceBook: www.eliminatechaos.com/facebook

Bonus material and resources can be found at www.eliminate thechaosatwork.com.

Index